Blessings
William
Sept 2001

What's God Got to Do with It?

William E. Perry, Jr.

Copyright © 2000 by William E. Perry, Jr.

All rights reserved. No part of this book shall be reproduced or transmitted in any form or by any means, electronic, mechanical, magnetic, photographic including photocopying, recording or by any information storage and retrieval system, without prior written permission of the publisher. No patent liability is assumed with respect to the use of the information contained herein. Although every precaution has been taken in the preparation of this book, the publisher and author assume no responsibility for errors or omissions. Neither is any liability assumed for damages resulting from the use of the information contained herein.

ISBN 0-7414-0555-5

Cover design by Cathi A. Wong
Published by:

Infinity Publishing.com
519 West Lancaster Avenue
Haverford, PA 19041-1413
Info@buybooksontheweb.com
www.buybooksontheweb.com
Toll-free (877) BUY BOOK
Local Phone (610) 520-2500
Fax (610) 519-0261

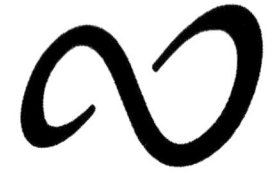

Printed in the United States of America
Printed on Recycled Paper
Published December-2000

Acknowledgment

The value of interdependent relationships (the healthy ones) can never be underestimated during such crazy times as writing a book. Why would I single out this time as particularly crazy? The answer is simple. The creative expression is screaming to be released, while the loose ends keep piling up, chapter by chapter. For me, writing is one thing; editing is another. Both are necessary for a creative, flowing, intelligible manuscript. Thankfully the Universe sent me some wonderful support in the form of "human angels" who helped me expand my efforts to achieve an internally acceptable form.

Without the likes of Jo Ann Hartley, this book would still be stuck in my computer waiting for edification.

edification

ed i fi ca tion [èdd⎕fi káysh'n] *noun*

enlightenment: instruction or enlightenment, especially when it is morally or spiritually uplifting[1]

In my humble opinion she followed this dictionary definition to the letter. For me, any uplift and enlightment this book may contain were either enhanced or created because of Jo Ann and her brilliant instructions.

My heartfelt thanks also go out to Nanci White whose masterful editing added magic, spice, and clarity to the forthcoming pages. She knew just how to steer me out of confusion and into the light of creativity.

Bill Elias, you were, have been and will always be an angel to me. Your steady encouragement and ongoing dedication to my work are a constant inspiration. Thank you for all of your suggestions and steady input, both with the content as well as my vision for this book.

---

[1] *Encarta® World English Dictionary* © & (P) 1999 Microsoft Corporation. All rights reserved. Developed for Microsoft by Bloomsbury Publishing Plc.

And last but not least, I want to acknowledge Tom Jones. In my opinion, he is Palm Beach's most friendly postal employee, exemplifying more than anyone around me the fine art of serving. This man is the epitome of someone who loves his job and serves his customers with impeccable attention, kindness and dedication. If the whole world were like Tom, it would surely be a more peaceful place. Thank you for being a constant inspiration for my writing.

Preface

What's God Got to Do with It? The answer to this question is quite simple: "Everything." This book is devoted to the stories that can lead to empowerment through the inclusion of God in every decision and action. In my years as a mental health counselor, pastoral counselor, minister, and spiritual director, I have discovered the importance of spiritual development in daily life. I am convinced that to be sane mentally, stable emotionally, and fit physically, we must honor our spiritual nature and the power of God available to us in every moment of our lives. My own life is a testament to this needed focus for by excluding it, I became broken and lifeless. With God in my life, there is more peace, contentment and excellent health than ever before. The joy of living and participating fully in my purpose was restored to me when I interjected spirituality into everyday decision making.

As a youngster I experienced very little division between the physical and nonphysical worlds. I was fully connected to supernatural guidance, the loving protection of Jesus, and total trust in the Almighty. As the wheels of socialization and education turned in my life, focus on these three blessings diminished with time until they were practically forgotten. The price for over-immersing myself in the material world was heavy and because of my stubbornness, it took a life challenging illness for me to return to my spiritual path. My confusion was further exacerbated because although I was active in practicing my religious life, I was not keen to the need for spiritual reconnection and grounding. Trust me; there is a difference.

Spirituality, grounded in all major religions, asks in part that we reconnect with our mystical roots and search for the truth. It is far less interested in adherence to a path and more interested in helping us seek our own. In essence, spirituality is here to help us liberate, live wholeheartedly, and experience the bliss of freedom. Finding and living the truth of God in every moment is the message of this book. For me this quest has been not only life-enhancing, it has been the reason for my existence.

The following pages are about reconnection to Spirit using stories of real life struggles, psycho-spiritual awareness gained from them, and practical techniques to facilitate change. The estrangement with the supernatural world leaves a major void in the lives of countless millions. This manuscript is my attempt to remind us all of what God has to do with it! The "It" in my title is the journey itself. From birth to death we are essentially spiritual beings constantly struggling to remember our origin and roots. We struggle because we have been taught that the mind and emotions are all that's needed to achieve excellence, success and happiness. The clients you read about, as well as myself, are living proof to the contrary. Only by remembering that each of us has a unique purpose and that we all have a God to help us find and follow that purpose can we fill the void in life.

I have purposely chosen to call God by many other names to remind us of the omniscient, omnipotent, omnipresent essence of our Creator. These names are also to remind all of us, especially myself, that God will always remain a constant source of mystery. They are in no way used to indicate irreverence or defiance towards traditional religious practices. Enjoy your journey.

Introduction

I believe there is an inherent need in the hearts of each of us to know and feel more sincerely the Creative Force that is responsible for our makeup. This book is my attempt to share some human experiences, including my own, which have been instrumental, even if negatively at times, in making individuals accessible to Divine Wisdom and its benefits in daily life. The magnificent power of God constantly flows in and around each of us. Access to this natural, awe-inspiring Force can be given top priority with patience, practice and perseverance. Firsthand accounts of individuals who attempted to exclude this omniscient power are recounted again and again in hopes that the reader takes the initiative to follow some of the simple, practical, yet oh-so-effective exercises suggested at the end of strategic chapters. So if you're willing to come along for an adventure into practical spirituality for the 21st century, sit back, open your mind, and enjoy.

Table of Contents

Chapter	Page

One:
Practical Spirituality 1

Two:
Higher Ground 9

Three:
Sacred Texts: A Doorway To Truth 14

Four:
Feelings Are Extremely Useful 21

Five:
Anger 27

Six:
Pain 36

Seven:
Relationships 44

Eight:
Spiritual Partnerships 53

Nine:
What Do I Deserve? 60

Ten:
Preplanning Your Life 68

Eleven:
Say "Yes" to Life by Identifying Your Choices 73

Twelve:
If You Can't Say Something Positive, Remain Silent 81

Thirteen:
Being vs. Doing 85

Fourteen:
Monitor What Persists 92

Fifteen:
Practice Giving from the Heart 96

Sixteen:
Make It Light 101

Seventeen:
Refresh Your Body 104

Eighteen:
Give More Than You Are Required 109
Nineteen:
Practice Nonverbal Communication 114
Twenty:
Safety 120
Twenty-One:
Equality: Think This Way Always 125
Twenty-Two:
Prerequisites to Manifestation 129
Twenty-Three:
How to Manifest 133
Twenty-Four:
Look to Nature 138
Twenty-Five:
Ultimate Forgiveness 148
Twenty-Six:
Quality of Life 153

Chapter One

Practical Spirituality

"The most beautiful thing we can experience is the mysterious."

-Albert Einstein

This book is the product of a lifelong study in spirituality. Most of us are busy trying to live comfortably. Comfort and spirituality have a lot in common, yet spirituality leads us home. We are most uncomfortable when we aren't at home with ourselves. There are two kinds of selves that we must deal with during the course of a lifetime. The first self contains the definition that we have given to our own unique individuality. This includes credit given to all that we stand for and have accomplished. Yet there is another Self; it contains our spiritual essence and definitions that stretch far beyond our control or recognition. These definitions are not ours alone for they belong mainly to our Creator.

The most important person to be attuned to in any given moment is our essential Self. The Spirit wants only that we should awaken its assets. When we remember to listen to the inner voice, dysfunction subsides and we return to a place that lulls us into harmony. The most common mistake made pertains to the art of forgetting. We're groomed in this great persuasion from birth.

I have written this book because I am convinced of the importance of spiritual discipline. When I follow these simple, yet effective, principles, all life changes for me. "What can I do?" has always been the question I've heard myself ask. I have found many answers; I now choose to share the most important ones with you.

Focus on the awesome power of the mind, emotions and intuitive feelings is most important. This combination leads to the art of remembering. What we remember most is how

1

the love for our powerful potential or soulfulness becomes the great quest. I know this human frustration because forgetting has created dilemmas shared by thousands of my clients over the years.

We must strive to remember what is important when we follow the spiritual disciplines. We are asked to come from a place of knowing what's inside of us. God is not involved in our path other than having condoned our right to have one. The spiritual path is a unique endeavor, a return to the awareness of the Creator's creation [our essence] while we are still in human form. We are here to create a life following the principles of free will, a special and unique gift bestowed upon us all. The most valid precept concerning free will is this: each of us has it and there are no exceptions to this fact.

There are basically two distinct approaches when it comes to following spiritual disciplines. The first centers on God as a force that demands allegiance. This precept encourages us to be fearful of the God Force. By the same token, we are encouraged to define God as love. A stranger to religion might find this first approach somewhat paradoxical and find the need to discipline himself or herself to appease a God who already loves us a waste of energy. I find the second approach to disciplining myself spiritually far more useful. When I do it, not for the sake of my God but for the sake of my sanity and health, the discipline becomes far more enlivening. We each know that encoded within us is the secret formula to ensure human success. Each of us is equipped with inner knowing, which promotes safety, compassion, and health in every situation of our lives. It is the latter approach to spirituality that we shall cover in this text.

In order to legitimize the spiritual path and have a valid reason to follow the spiritual disciplines, we must ask the question, "Where will this lead me?" The answer to this question is strikingly simple: toward self-realization.

We also come face to face with a universal truth. Nothing outside of us is responsible for our actions or us. This statement lies to rest any controversy surrounding victimization. The illusion of victimhood is predicated on the reality that humans are capable of being enslaved by their own beliefs.

Beliefs are established in three primary ways. First of all, we invent them in our fantasy world. It is important to realize we each came to planet Earth to uncover a flaw in our character by discovering truth. These flaws represent spaces of alienation between our Creator and us. Our higher universal nature would like to eliminate this separation or gap. Fantasizing separation from God is at the center of this way of formulating beliefs.

The second way that beliefs are created is by our exposure to the environment. We, under our misguided volition, alienate ourselves from the Source by creating limiting fearful thoughts about the world around us. Many of these thoughts are of a religious nature. I can remember, as a child in Sunday school, being reminded again and again that God would punish me for my sins; obviously the concept of original sin was being passed down one more time. The lack of nurturing and physical contact that went on in my family encouraged me to believe, even if on a subconscious level, that human closeness must not be right or ordinary. As a child I was exposed to a condemning view of the body, especially the erotic parts, because my parents told me that these places were untouchable and their exploration was "nasty." My religious instructors warned me that the flesh was nothing more than a temptation device and that very little had changed since the temptation in the Garden of Eden.

The third way that we operate from our beliefs is by failing to recognize that the subconscious ones primarily rule our lives. By default we let powerful beliefs in our subconscious reign over us. Default comes about when we fail to observe the patterns that establish the negative traditions of our lives. Once recognized we have the power to know what needs to be changed in us in order to live more effectively. In a flash, at any age, anyone is capable of establishing a new belief, which can remain throughout his or her life. The motivator for this quick change of mind is often fear. Fear can be effective, but this question must always be asked, "Does this fear-based decision create a more healthy, loving me?" Our personal responsibility at present is to reprogram what no longer serves us as useful.

The concept of belief, established prior to our birth, is alien to many of us. It is my experience, as one who can communicate with the Spirit world, that lessons continue on both sides of the veil. If we live an existence that fortifies a central theme that is contrary to love, then it establishes a fatal flaw within.

Love, which is the action side of Creator, desires to be expressed in every situation. If a person establishes a set of beliefs in a particular life that promotes bigotry, then a future life is established to work on this theme.

The environment in which a person is reared can foster the predisposition towards hatred of a particular race or lifestyle. We can see the progression of formed beliefs yet the roots are often established well before birth. Each person has the ability to move past a predisposition to think in certain ways, overcome the thought patterns of a negative environment, and retrain the subconscious by using a few simple re-programming techniques.

Victimhood feeds upon itself. Whenever this definition has been taken on by anyone towards himself or herself, he or she immediately starts seeking reinforcement for this invented illusion. The subconscious mind demands allegiance to its belief, whatever it is. If the belief happens to be the need to receive negative attention or an excuse not to take personal responsibility for one's life, then the victim role seems quite appropriate. The victim will often steer any conversation towards his or her dilemma, demanding sympathy and an audience to vent distrust, anger, and frustration.

The most spiritually enlightened refuse to participate in this game. Instead they lovingly steer the conversation to what is healthy, productive, or useful. If we choose to feel sorry for anyone, we are ultimately reinforcing our doubts about our own, as well as his or her, ability to succeed. The victim chooses to take no responsibility for what appears to be tragedy. The question, "Why is this happening to me?", often surfaces, yet a real answer is never sought.

A healthy identity outside the victim role is often so unfamiliar that humans who have milked an unhealthy identity often cringe with fear when it is challenged. Spirituality, like psychotherapy, challenges us always to face our fears. Fears are often alienation from God's grace. I try to share with my clients the existence of subconscious drivers that often bring about the feeling of debilitation.

These drivers are so engrained that to the believer they seem real. The most important thing that we can learn about a belief is this amazing fact--they can, and must, be changed constantly in order to live a successful spiritual life. The victim often spiels out his message of "I can't" in rapid-fire succession. What he is really saying is, "I choose not to change; I want to be identified as a victim and I like all the negative attention I can generate."

Spirituality would ask us to transfer our awareness of what we think we are doing to what we are really doing. By saying, "I can't," I am asking the world to excuse me from taking possession of and responsibility for my life. Simply put, things are happening to me because I choose them. A simple shift in perception can save me hours, days, or even months of agonizing torture and frustration when trying to figure out why life is going astray.

The gift of change is scary for most people for two main reasons. Looking bad during the process freezes certain individuals in place. The mind shudders with the consequences of possibly making a mistake. Spiritually speaking, the only real mistake we can make is that of omission. Failure to take a risk and try something new becomes the noticeable harm. The challenge is to be honest and to ask the only pertinent question, "What is wrong with trying?"

I was recently in a restaurant with some friends and acquaintances. One member of our party looked at the menu and declared, "There's nothing on this menu I can eat." In that powerful instant, he declared, "Change is far too risky and unpredictable." His love of self vanished in that very second, because his menu choices were reduced to zero.

My friend believed this; "I have no choice." In his mind, he had no choice because should he pick something that was not edible, in his perception, he would have looked like a fool to the whole table. He did not want to sit there avoiding a huge plate of food because it did not match his taste buds. By comparison, the risk factor here would have been small. By accepting the possibility of making a mistake and the possibility of a few wasted "bucks," he may have started the beginning of a lifelong relationship with a new and very pleasing ethnic dish.

The second reason that change creates fear is because we are dealing with the future where there is no known point of reference. We are not there yet; therefore, we are not able to accurately predict the outcome of a chosen path. When a belief system is predicated on the idea that life is out to get us, life becomes scary. As children we are told to be cautious, dubious, and cynical of anyone who appears to be different. This comes from a false idea that sameness breeds protection. The repetition of patterns, such as always ordering the same dish in a restaurant, gives the illusion of protection yet it ensures nothing concerning the future. Food poisoning, a new chef, inferior quality produce or meat could all become variables in dealing with the future of a good meal. The most useful protection in life is trusting what the heart knows. Even though we train the brain to believe in fear, the heart knows better. By focusing on love and respect for ourselves, we soon align with a higher truth. We show this love most effectively when we are undertaking the adventures of life by moving past rigid points of view, repeated patterns, and useless safeguards.

We have memory of all events. Some reside in the subconscious and are relegated to long-term memory; the rest we can remember consciously. If we have been involved in an event that proved itself harmless, we become desensitized and fearless. Remembering these times can bolster our courage and foster our ability to take chances. Remembering capability and how it can pay off in the creation and pursuit of a goal is essential in finding the courage to overcome early indoctrination and false notions about what is safe or unsafe.

A return to innocence is the most hoped for place any spiritual pilgrim can connect with. Innocence overcomes both the fear of unacceptability and the unknown. We can never go back to the place of pre-indoctrination, but we can rewrite our belief system to align ourselves with Divine Union. This energy is always exploring, expanding, moving forward exponentially into life with one single conviction: **life is safe enough to be lived.** I trust these words and they have offered enormous relief in my life. The opinions of others that once had me shaking in my shoes subside more and more every day; I'm less dominated by the external need for approval and my control issues lessen because I'm able to trust the unknown as my ally and doorway to unfathomable expanses of adventure.

At one point in my life I would have felt sorry for the man in the restaurant who was afraid. I now hold onto a vision that we all can rise above our perceived limitations and fearful spaces so that we may be true to the vision of unconditional love. An incident like this, which I see everyday in myself and others, has convinced me of the importance of this book and others like it. They are of vital importance. Sharing messages—which set us free, foster internal peace, and help us remember how safe life can be--is of far greater importance to me than any waste of sympathy. I try now to be empathetic, which is akin to throwing a lifeline to a drowning person, instead of jumping into a turbulent sea that would most likely suck us both under.

Chapter Two

Higher Ground

"No one becomes really educated without pursuing some study in which he took no interest. It is part of our education to interest ourselves in subjects for which we have no aptitude."

-T.S. Eliot

I would like to explain the nature of spiritual disciplines as I comprehend them. All spiritual disciplines are either fear based or love based. Every time any of us undertakes one of these disciplines out of fear, the creation of lack begins. Translated, this means when our heart isn't in an activity, our love is bogus and we began to pay less and less attention to it. When our heart is involved in a positive spiritual undertaking, we feel excited about the discipline. Fear-based disciplines create drudgery and are time-consuming endeavors. When the discipline lacks excitement and joy, nothing much seems to come from the process, which is a clear indicator of a closed heart. When a heart is open the *still, small voice of truth* begins to come forth. In actuality, it is more than a voice, for the disciplines of every spiritual path lead to one main goal, a sense of communication with the Divine. We might feel the direction, hear it, or envision it. All are legitimate ways of comprehending Creator on our path to wholeness.

I believe the experience of living a spiritual life operates best when undertaken joyfully! The day of the punishing Creator is over. Life on our planet proves that it does not work. Such religions as Judaism, the Islamic faith, as well as Christianity, can overly stress the wrath of God. In cultures where these faiths abound, there is still plenty of internal strife, lack of brotherly love, and lots of crime. Religious perspectives which encourage us to be fearful have track records of proven failure. Other, more positive religions, such as Taoism, Buddhism and Hinduism, likewise can be slow in showing gains when it comes to ushering in world peace. I believe it is time for change. Spirituality based on the joy and willingness of disciplining ourselves can be the new salvation. We have observed the heavy-handedness of martyrdom, mortification, and original sin without their accomplishing long-term success. I believe that a few thousand years of practice is an adequate test run to measure the usefulness of fear-based spiritual disciplines.

Those who would remain blind to this reality out of allegiance to a faith lose in the long run for they deny themselves the rewards of a joyful, love-based life. How many wars have been started in the name of religion, allowing man to justify his greed by mimicking an angry God? How much hate and human slaughter have come from the fear and repression of a vengeful God? In my experience with spiritual direction, I have observed countless clients who've given up believing in their redemption. They have so disciplined themselves to believe in their unworthiness that they give up in hopeless despair and go out and live the useless life. Those who believe that Creator has given up on them or that Creator is quick to punish or condemn them more easily do this to themselves and others. The pressure of living with the idea that God is always keeping score is often so rampant among believers that they believe it's useless to walk the straight and narrow because their sins are so great.

At this point many religious Christians would scream, "This is why the Savior has come." He has promised to restore us to health by forgiving our sins. My point is this: wouldn't it be easier to have a God exclusively of love in our corner so that we don't live in constant fear of displeasing Him? Wouldn't a God who never needed to forgive us because he never condemned us in the first place be more psychologically easy to comprehend and live with? The truth is *we do live with God everyday* and what we know of this Force by way of what we have been taught far outweighs what we know about Him from our hearts.

The primary job of any spiritual discipline is to lead us back to a relationship with the truth of God instead of trying to identify the one true God. The focus of all religious wars has involved this theme and is the subject of their justification. If we can train ourselves to think of Creator as having unconditional positive regard for our existence, then the experience of making a mistake becomes less condemning. In our conscious minds we normally have little regard for offenses against God, yet in our subconscious experience, in the hidden mind, great consternation often takes place. We forget how powerful our upbringing has been concerning the automatic decisions we make from the subconscious point of view. Thousands of automatic decisions pop up in us each hour, all based on early programming. If this program contains beliefs that we are constantly being scrutinized by a forceful, vengeful, easily-angered God, then our focus remains clearly pointed in the direction of a hangman's noose.

Following spiritual disciplines that come from love and a loving attitude towards the Divine Creator is the path we shall take from here. If you are interested in fear-based disciplines, there are volumes on the subject. As I have mentioned, they can be a constant source of pain and suffering in a believer's attempt to communicate with the loving God. In the following examples you'll notice a trend which tends to remove all tedious drudgery from the undertaking. This opens the door to legitimate steps of knowing and communicating with the Divine Mind on an extremely personal basis.

Christianity stresses a personal relationship with God through his son, Jesus Christ. I've been hard pressed to experience much in the way of exposure to genuine dialogue through my experience of growing up as Methodist and later converting to Catholicism. During my tenure as a pastoral counselor for the Catholic Church, I was amazed at how infrequently deep, personal communication with the Source was taught. A form of communication called prayer was primarily taught. It became a legitimate means of presenting our "laundry list" to God. The emphasis was usually on what God needed to do for us or what we should do, out of heavy obligation, for Him instead of discerning what might be appropriate or authentic in the type of service our Creator might really desire. I would prefer to be around those who practice legitimate discernment and know when to "pitch in" when I'm down and out instead of engaging in the fine art of proselytization which would only tend to aggravate me.

Knowing how to serve by way of high-level discernment is the goal I challenge you to consider. If these approaches sound radical then I encourage you to live with the shakeup in your mind, for it is the first step in changing outdated beliefs. Resistance is always an indicator of the ego's asking you to remain stagnant and retain your present beliefs without question. When resistance arrives, look at it as a mark of your progress and a real sign of growth!

To justify exposure to the spiritual disciplines ahead, ask yourself one question, "Can I trust my present communication with the Divine Source to be a legitimate means of receiving authentic direction for my life?"

My students have often asked me, "When is the best time to utilize a spiritual discipline?" So many people have been taught to communicate with God only when there is a dire need. This constitutes the only condition for prayer for millions of religious devotees. One-way communication might work for religion, but it is limited in scope when it comes to the vast potential of knowing what a deep inner path to spirituality stresses. I believe the **best** times to undertake a spiritual discipline are these: No. 1) when Divine Intelligence calls; No. 2) when you are **not** doing it out of obligation; No. 3) when you want to solicit God's grace by staying with the quest lovingly until resolution appears; No. 4) when you are **not** stressed out, anxious or in a hurry for relief.

It is easy to become attached to the outcome of relief when we beseech the spiritual disciplines. The object becomes one more quick fix in our repertoire of instant relief. If anyone is feeling sorry for himself and wants God's help, it usually corresponds to a time when the attachment to the outcome is so high, relief is often blocked. It is far better to ask ourselves one simple question. "In this moment of distress how can I serve humanity?" After receiving a legitimate answer, find the courage to go out and undertake the task. Within a short time you return to stability and an inner sense of usefulness and fulfillment. Why does this phenomenon occur? Because any time the universal precepts are initiated, especially in times of imbalance and disharmony, the result is a return to love, internal peace, and mental stability. The truth in question is this: giving and receiving are the same. In this case, giving time and attention outside one's need for self-pity yields a feeling of internal worth, raised self-esteem, and personal satisfaction for choosing to help another. One quickly moves out of the doldrums by following this simple formula.

How do you know when Divine Intelligence is encouraging you to follow a discipline? A "spring into action" is felt at your core, as if you were sitting in the cockpit of a jet fighter and had just pushed the eject button. In this image you can feel yourself thrust forward, high above, and out of the way of the aircraft. You then feel the pull of the ripcord, the parachute opening and a slow descent to earth. There is no other feeling like this one; an invincibility and courage preside simultaneously. You hit eject and all you can do is spring forward. Thought gets out of the way and in its wake powerful feelings of assurance, even if fleeting, take over. The experience, no matter how you try to rationalize it, cannot be denied.

Try this previously outlined exercise. It can be humbling, yet know that with patience and an assured loving attitude, important communication with the Divine will emerge. Honor that it becomes easier when you're not in the state of anxiety and panic over needing your prayers answered your way, right away.

Chapter Three

Sacred Texts: A Doorway to Truth

"Spiritual genius emerges from every facet of God's diamond. All faith traditions share his light."

-Marianne Williamson

It is easy to stay focused and in a positive mood when dissatisfaction with life is minimized. In times of struggle it is harder to bounce back to a place of harmony. A most useful tool when things are going poorly is to have enlightened material handy. Read it, re-read it, contemplate its message, and read it again. I like discerning the wisdom in such books as the *I Ching, Book of Changes*. The revelation factor is amazing, always informative and pertinent to my uneasiness. I've often been questioned about the use of discernment material and its validity, so I would like to share the following insights. If I'm looking for something to tell me exactly what to do, I'm forfeiting my job as a pilgrim on the higher consciousness path. If I'm looking for forgotten pieces of my puzzle and insight that bring me closer to my truth, then any form of divination becomes spiritually sound and useful.

Alignment with truth is a permanent quest contiguous to humanity. Millions stay oblivious and remain ignorant of this fact yet it is what we do in life. Each of us is looking to reclaim alignment with, and allegiance to, our Spirit. This disconnection represents the loss of Paradise, the forgotten Shangri-La. All human spirit has direct access to our truth. The simplest way of knowing truth is this; concerning a desired outcome, it is the clearest, most useful, and ultimately rewarding vision we can hold. Let me give you an example. I was talking to a fourteen-year-old, super bright young man named Edward.[2] When I explained to him that the criticism he so fluidly and vehemently launched against his brother was a statement of how he really felt about himself, he laughed uproariously. Edward's vision of himself is completely different from his truth. Every word uttered against another has a correlation aspect to it. Each time any of us speaks harshly against someone, an aspect of our negative opinion of ourselves appears, revealing a secret agenda. In this case, Edward fails to embrace highly or lovingly condone his performance in life. He remains blind to this reality. It is not important that he understands what I attempted to explain to him; what is important is that he ultimately realizes how life on this planet operates. The ongoing truths of humanity are so simple they are often overlooked and denigrated to a status of impractical, oversimplified or stupid platitudes by highly thinking individuals.

Universal Truths[3] are so simple, self evident, and uncomplicated they seem at first implausible, almost useless.

---

[2] The stories that I present here are true but not necessarily factual. Some characteristics of people in the stories are a composite of many past clients. Truth lies in the message of a story, its empowering content, and how well it shares some aspect of Universal Truth. The names of characters in this and every chapter forthcoming have been changed to protect the confidentiality agreement between counselor and client.
[3] Universal Truths are the building blocks of the universe. Isaac Newton, who is more known as a scientist than a metaphysician, actually spent most of his life bridging the gap between spirituality and physical science by discovering the metaphysical laws and then discovering parallel applications in the physical world. His definition of the premier Universal building block is taught to every beginning science student. It states that for every action there is an equal and opposite reaction. Upon this law (cause and effect) all universal principals are built. The subsets of this law include the principals of manifestation, giving and receiving, everything has a purpose, and the law of least effort. Christian Scripture, for example, would state the laws this ways: "Whatever we give out, we will have it multiplied back to us" (Luke 5: 38); "As a man thinketh in his heart so he is" (Proverbs 23:7); "Whatsoever things you desire, when you pray, believe that ye will receive them, and ye shall have them" (Mark 11:24); "God has not given you a spirit of fear but of love and power and a sound mind" (II Timothy 1:7); "Do not have any anxieties, do not have any stress. Do not allow it in your thinking"

15

Imagine how hard it is for someone who has never been taught the validity of truths to practice them in daily problem solving. Each of us butts our heads against the wall of illusion until we decide to break it down. When I experience those who come to me for counseling, stuck in states of panic, distress, or hopelessness, it is evident these signs represent ongoing, lifelong resistance. The resistance is towards acceptance of personal as well as Universal Truth. It amazes me to see myself and others continually crash because of stubborn beliefs, which we refuse to change. When I experience people in crisis, I try to help them rejoice in their situation for some part of them is reaching out, searching for the courage to follow the Universal Way, any way that uses the Universal Truths as its core. The Universal Way is part of the foundation of all the world's major religions.

One of the most puzzling dilemmas for any spiritual seeker is the perceived problem of maintaining one's spiritual nature and disciplines around those who have no interest in the subject of transformation or spiritual evolution. I remind you that regardless of the degree of awareness an individual has regarding his or her spiritual journey, he or she is undertaking one nonetheless. This reality is an inescapable part of human consciousness. Under scrutiny, who can deny that a spirit drives us? The spirits of ambition, conquest, desire, longing, greed, intrigue or understanding are constantly being explored by even the most self-declared unspiritual being. The spirit is a *nature* that is greater than the physical, mental, or emotional self. It is pure feeling, which, at our core, we are all made of. When we are in our deepest, most natural feeling mode, the Spirit of us comes alive reminding us of our sacred being, which loves experiencing its own truth.

This clue, the importance of feeling Spirit, is what seekers are looking for when it comes to maintaining a spiritual

---

(Matthew 6); "Let my words be few" (Ecclesiastes 5:2); "Speak the truth in love" (II Timothy 4:2).

focus out in the world. Instead of feeling isolated when companions on the journey are absent, one can learn *how to center* in the midst of chaos and confusion. It is easier to know a personal, God, Creator, Creation, to experience the feelings of who we are, and let our Spirits soar when we are in prayer, contemplation, or meditation. It is just as easy to train ourselves to know truth while in the midst of all kinds of external chaotic stimuli. There are two main keys in understanding this phenomenon. Number one, you *can* be in two places at one time. One can be in the world, grounded and physical while being beyond the world in the feeling and value of God. Number two, decide to pay close attention to the uneasiness experienced in your thoughts and feelings, for it will show you when your attention is no longer focused on spiritual growth. Each of us knows instinctively when we have violated the principles of truth contained within both higher self and the Universe.

The primary *truth* surrounding the human condition is this. "Life is a paradox to be accepted and understood as a mystery during this lifetime." Why do people who want to be good act badly? Why do bad things happen to good people? Why can't we just decide to change our behavior and then do it? Why, if we've been taught that God is love, do we then observe this same Force playing havoc with our planet? Why do we so easily find fault with ourselves and life around us, instead of looking at the good and praising it? Why do we proclaim, "I want to be prosperous and enriched by healthy relationships," only to fall in the trap of struggle and co-dependency? This list of paradoxical interactions we have towards our wishes, hopes, and dreams and the world at large goes on and on and on. The main activity needed to understand *truth* is the practice of accepting these mysteries to the best of our ability.

Fortunately those who begin to discover the mechanics of life also begin to eliminate personal victimhood and perceived limitations as well. The greatest discovery surrounding personal truth is this: each of us has unlimited potential to succeed. The focus of our success is an individual matter and can change according to free will. Each human being on earth is unencumbered the moment he or she adopts this stance concerning ultimate freedom; "Freedom's just another word for nothing left to lose" goes the line of a famous Kristofferson song. This *truth* has been defined in hundreds of different ways; I'm only sharing here my particular preference. In this one clear statement, the concept of "thou shall have no other gods before me" becomes real. It is a path to freedom, totally universal and totally applicable to every situation the mind can conceive. When the mind attaches itself to an outrageous outcome regarding a person, place, or thing, thus creating an addictive nature, truth steps in and demands our awareness, which will show us the folly of our false god. Success is in direct proportion to a desired outcome.

Unlimited success always has this prerequisite: if I want something I can't live without and must have, I'm creating a false god. The truth is: "I can live without what I must have including my own physical life." The Divine Creator, Universal Intelligence, Savior, Creator, Christ Consciousness, Higher Power (whatever you want to call God) wants us to understand the lesson of ultimate allegiance. A lesson is created for us whereby lasting, rewarding, success is <u>denied</u> until we return to the fold and stop obsessing over our attachment. Honoring a personally chosen true God is the ultimate path, for the moment we adopt this precept nothing can stand in our way. "Why?" you ask. The answer is simple. Humans lack the desire to focus on perfect timing, which causes them to be either lazy or overly zealous concerning their goals. Humans lack the training and foresight to focus on the past, present and future simultaneously, which is precisely what God does for us.

Once help is solicited, reaching out to God's infinite wisdom and utilizing it to achieve a goal bring us back into perfect alignment with the Universal Flow. In this moment of surrender, <u>unlimited potential</u> is felt in every cell of our being, in every strand of consciousness and in the purest place of the heart. When we detach from an outcome, hold fast to our belief that we are deserving, and give full allegiance to the Divine Creator, any goal can be achieved.

As you can see, unlimited potential has a prerequisite—detachment--which is at the heart of all struggle. Giving up an attachment is the main criteria for that special person who wants to move out of poverty and into healthy relationships. It is the elixir for all smooth behavioral changes and it explains why we don't get what we proclaim we want. Each reminder that lovingly and gently guides us towards the truth becomes a welcome addition to our discernment repository.

The past, present and future are all experienced simultaneously in spirit. When our attention lovingly glides towards a glimmer of what has been true in the past, is relevant in the moment, and is imperative for future dreams to be realized, we are in the flow. Imagine a continual stream of consciousness that knows all; now imagine the usefulness of this information. Garnering information that will glean one shining example of what path is most true for us can yield great results. Energy output can be reduced, experimentation can be eliminated, and plain old trial-and-error becomes obsolete. Why? Because the best and most useful path has been pre-ordained. All we need to do is be open to this free flow of information that can show us the glorious road to freedom.

Books transcribed by sages, prophets and spiritual pilgrims contain multitudinous examples of Universal Truths. The laws that govern the universe are explained over and over in the *Bible*, the *Tibetan Book of the Dead*, the *Kabala*, the *Koran*, and recent works such as *Conversations with God* or *The Seven Spiritual Laws of Success*. When our patience runs thin and connection to the flow runs dry, a quick trip to one of these references can bring us back to the fold. We can easily remember the law of cause and effect, the rules of manifestation, the meaning of detachment, the truth of projection and the correlation between giving and receiving with the flip of a page and a focus of attention. Discernment is unlimited, bound by no particular religion or dogma. God speaks to all his children, all the time, so whether we receive it through personal awareness or through a message that has come before makes very little difference. The essence of truth is beyond time and space and is always ready to give us an audience. It is up to us to believe in the miracle of this gift, have faith in its healing power, and find the courage to use it when we are heartsick, lonely, or scared.

You'll know in your heart of hearts if a message is right for you. After you consult sacred texts conduct a feeling check to see if it is speaking to you or not. If it does, be open, take heart, rejoice and ponder the message it is trying to convey-- a message of pertinent and perfect guidance for the moment that is at hand. Remember your special ally; Sacred Truth found in sacred texts is easily accessible even when things are going poorly.

Chapter Four

Feelings Are Extremely Useful

"The young man who has not wept is a savage. The old man who will not laugh is a fool."

-George Santayana

Each of us has a basic need to move in the direction of our highest good. The way we know this direction is by feeling it. We feel a prompting, an inner-urge that goes beyond short-term gain or instant gratification. If we decide for no other reason to register feelings, this one stands out as paramount. To feel is a sublime recognition of Universal Presence. God comes to humans first and foremost through their feeling function. Feelings provide a direct pipeline to the awareness of God or Universal Presence. To honor and comprehend the message of this Presence brings higher order to our lives. Stop every time you and your feelings are divorced, make a conscious decision to change direction, and began feeling life once again. Automatic adjustment of our radar will begin to take place so that detection of the next most valuable decision can be felt from deep within.

So often the *feeling* experience of life is disavowed by the world of *practicality*. This camouflage is created because of the anxiety surrounding risk-taking. Individuals who perceive themselves as weak, vulnerable, and ripe for attack relegate the world of feelings to **dangerous territory**. Whenever consciousness drifts there, either automatically or through a series of high-strung events, panic starts to take over. To counteract these feelings, which are trying to be avoided like the plague, rational, well formulated, articulate thought is chosen. At this point the individual begins to play a trick on himself or herself. The more he or she tries to avoid feelings the more he or she slides between the cracks of consciousness and enters the dreaded experience. It is only understood this way because feelings have been defined as irrelevant and a nuisance to those who want to "get on with their lives."

Kevin is such a person; he wants life to be picture perfect and full of ease and elegance. Spirituality shows us that life can be this way, but shifts in attitude must take precedence. The first shift comes when acceptance overrides the need to judge harshly. The second shift occurs when the need to be right gives way to the internal need to stay active. Active individuals are taking what they want from life's data bank, focusing less on the trap of mental scrutiny, by deciding less and less what should be *right*. The third shift constitutes a willingness to explore new use and definition of the familiar. Humans slot and peg everything surrounding them, thinking, "I know what this is good for and how it *should* be used." Choosing to embrace the full spectrum of a situation can be a remarkably powerful gift.

Kevin likes avoidance. He attempts to avoid the sticky, messy, gooey side of life every time he fails to engage his feelings. He has convinced himself that this area is poison and needs avoiding. Kevin simply says, "I've had enough." The belief falsely accelerates an attempt to take control of his life by reinforcing "no more of this garbage." The garbage, according to Kevin, is anyone's decision that would cause an adverse emotional reaction within him. If his girlfriend chooses to be with her daughter instead of him it causes a negative emotional reaction. Jealousy ensues and it bothers Kevin because she has made the conscious decision to be with another instead of him. The trap for Kevin is that he likes relationships, especially with his girlfriend, and wants to be with her. At the same time he wants her to be available to him at all times and when she is not, feelings of an insecure nature arise. At this point Kevin would just as soon not be in relationship as be in it because the unknown factor of her perceived allegiance drives him crazy.

Consequently, avoidance creeps in primarily because Kevin, unknown to his conscious mind, starts creating distance between himself and his beloved. He either criticizes her, which causes her withdrawal, or works himself into a frenzy emotionally which causes his withdrawal because she can no longer be trusted. Instead of accomplishing his goal to sidestep the sticky, gooey side of life, Kevin ends up right where he doesn't want to be in the midst of an unpleasant situation spawning unpleasant emotions. In truth his actions have avoided nothing. It becomes clear spiritually that *avoidance* is a trap. Whatever defenses an individual puts up to avoid something pales in comparison to the creative capacity of the Universe. It soon becomes evident on a secret level of consciousness how ludicrous the endeavor to outsmart God (Universal Intelligence) really is. The Universe in her infinite ability to expand is no match for our wits. All avoidance is a clear indicator that fear is at hand. Creator wants us to know how fearless we can be, so over and over again we are given opportunities to prove to others and ourselves how courageous the human spirit really is.

When Kevin craves avoidance he prolongs his lessons which sends out a signal to the universe, "We have a hard head on our hands." Stubborn, resistant, stuck individuals are on earth to remember that with faith, focus, and courage all unspiritual, unfounded fears can ultimately disappear. The more Kevin avoids the truth, the more intense his lessons become. I can only speculate concerning the ultimate reason why. My conclusion is that life is like school and each person is bound to learn lessons while attending. The Headmaster wants each student to know the benefits of higher consciousness and the ultimate power that lies within the human framework. This Great Scholar wants all of those in his school to know that **truth will set you free** and that freedom is the ultimate weapon against fear. The Headmaster wants to pass down the wisdom of the ages so that each student knows how to be the ultimate success story and acquire his heart's desire. This Sage knows the direction called *up* is attained only when the fear of falling down subsides. Kevin fears being the sole decision maker in his life, that his opinions of himself are not enough, and that he needs the bolstering effect of family, friends, employees and lovers to identify him adequately. This gifted young man avoids the truth while at the same time the Universe in her divine wisdom longs for him to remember. She chooses to help him every step along the way and she does so in the most beneficial ways. [It is my firm conviction that the Divine Creator is both male and female, as well as everything else, simultaneously. I purposely interchange gender identification to stress the omniscience of God.] She shows us the opposite of truth in every instance. It is registered in our feelings of discomfort and agitation. Kevin ignores these feelings so they come to him again and again in the form of physical discomfort and emotional distress. Why is the Universe doing this? Primarily because she loves him and wants Kevin to remember his truth.

If the Headmaster knows what will make his students content and peaceful, it is his obligation to pass this knowledge on to them. God gives Kevin this opportunity daily. Kevin's avoidance at present is this. He believes that others know more about what is good for him than he does, thus ranking their opinions above his own. Yet each time this happens, something snaps and recoils inside of this man and he automatically becomes defensive and starts proclaiming, "Why are they trying to tell me what to do?" The answer is simple, because constantly, on a telepathic, subconscious level, he is encouraging them to do just that. His weaker side is screaming for reinforcement because he fears wrong decisions and consequently looking like a fool. His controlling nature proclaims him to be a free agent in life, not to be messed with by others. The Universe wants him to be free to make decisions, not from a standpoint of the defense fueled by control issues, but instead from a loving heart where he is in tune with the Headmaster on a constant basis.

What is a practical application concerning the three vital shifts in attitude that Kevin can make to ensure comfort in life and how are they tied to his emotional stability? The body automatically feels lack of acceptance each time Kevin obsesses about his girlfriend's whereabouts, so the first thing he can do is stop long enough to register these feelings. The next thing he can do is remember to mentally categorize the feelings he is experiencing. Are they feelings of truth or are they fear based? Kevin can now go down a mental checklist to ascertain the difference. Truth feelings are accompanied by a sense of expansion and unlimited capability to overcome. Acceptance of the situation is more than a mental undertaking; it includes warm, soothing, comforting feelings. Acceptance destroys the need to pass negative judgment by focusing on what is important in the moment. What is necessary for Kevin to maintain acceptance? He needs continual registration of the feelings surrounding acceptance in order to put negative judgment to rest.

The place of harsh critical judgment never sits well in human consciousness. The primary reason is because it is foreign to our spiritual nature. Kevin, therefore, has the ability to remember and re-enact feelings of being spiritual or succumb to the mental persuasion to relentlessly judge. As you can see, there is absolutely no avoidance of feelings in this process. There is, though, an immediate discipline to mentally focus on the most pertinent feelings. The discipline shifts from thinking in judgmental ways to the focusing on feelings that naturally come from accepting ways. The feelings are always there buried under layers and layers of what *should be*. Kevin was taught that he should be jealous; deep inside in his heart of hearts he knows the truth of tolerance, understanding, and forgiveness.

The second part of Kevin's exercise is to remember the gift of activity. My instruction to Kevin was this: "Ask yourself what it is you really want to do instead of challenging another person or group's definition of what is right." All Kevin needs to do in this moment is release his terrible stuckness by declaring, "There are as many *right* ways of doing something as there are minds involved in the process." The first activity is for Kevin to challenge his own belief system and ask his deepest sensing nature in what direction he feels like going. The action of engaging in the deepest desires of the heart always yields astounding results. The last part of Kevin's exercise, as well as for anyone who wants to attune himself or herself, is this; each time a definitive thought declaring limited use or definition of some aspect of God's creation arises, lovingly ask, "What more can this matter be used for?" Add to this the question, "What power beyond my immediate comprehension exists here?"

Chapter Five

Anger

*"There is no greater illusion than fear,
No greater wrong than preparing to defend yourself,
No greater misfortune than having an enemy.
Whoever can see through all fear
Will always be safe."*

-Lao Tzu from <u>Tao Te Ching</u>,
translated by Stephen Mitchell

The most important aspect of anger is its use. **Anger is a natural emotional expression and is usually associated with fear.** Humans fear being overwhelmed by outside influences. Anger comes each time we deal with control issues, either internally or externally. Trying to control the world around us takes effort and can be draining physiologically and psychologically. Anger ensues because the internal strength to overcome resistance by the outside world is doubted. Each attempt to control what goes on around us is ongoing misguided effort, for in truth we control nothing but ourselves. A frequent rebuttal by workshop participants and clients usually goes like this, "How can that be?" My response is always the same, "What we have control over is our reaction, perception, and response to external stimuli." This is another example of the ever-present law of cause and effect. It reigns supreme in our world.

The need to control comes from a basic premise that life is unsafe and humans are ill equipped to handle a situation. These lies are taught to young, impressionable minds. They sometimes come from the minds and hearts of ill-informed, frightened teachers who come disguised as parents, peers, educators, or the law. I will never forget my second grade teacher who ridiculed me severely in class because she objected to the way I strolled back to my seat one day after a visit to the chalkboard. Her words penetrated me deeply, primarily because she was dealing with a very sensitive, easily hurt young boy. These traits in me were probably unknown and certainly undetected by her, yet anyone who works with a young, impressionable mind needs to be on diligent alert to the immediate and oftentimes lasting impact that a simple gesture of reprimand can offer. This woman wanted to control probably because she was having a difficult day managing the lives of twenty-four inquisitive, oftentimes wild, rambunctious youngsters. Yet this is never a good enough excuse to give the impression that someone is not capable of monitoring his or her long walk down the path of life. I will never know exactly why she needed to control me that day. Perhaps my walk looked stupid and she was trying to protect me from the opinions of twenty-three little critics. I will never know what prompted her to ridicule me, yet I do know the experience put a doubt in my mind as to how I personally should walk forward in life.

At least once a week I deal with well-intentioned parents who want to save their children from the hardships of life. Most often my clients have been through their own personal hells and know the scars and far reaching effect of these encounters. Still, to save an offspring from the lessons of life is a detriment. We learn by experience and every attempt to control another because of our fears violates the cosmic plan. Oftentimes my session is with the parent whose offspring is now an adult. It is my observation that not much has changed in the parent/child relationship since early childhood. The children are rebelling against the continued control of the parent even though they are quite capable of making a decision on their own. The problem is this: the adult child's solution is never good enough because the parent fears that he or she might still be subject to harm's way. After thousands of influencing situations, powerful beliefs are embedded in the thought patterns of a person. Control seems natural for anyone who feels ill equipped to handle not just life's challenging situations but everyday ones as well. If we have been belittled, berated, and chastised again and again, it is hard to imagine having the internal ability to solve everyday problems, let alone major issues, using the gifts of intuition and human intelligence. External control becomes the substitute of choice when doubt concerning personal power exists.

Another issue of concern focuses on what we think we are controlling in the first place. The term **situation** is probably the best description. Every situation of human value contains people, places, and things. The need to control any one or a combination of them stems from fear. Humans fear the loss of control because the expectation of always being right and successful plays such a major role in their thinking. According to our culture, a reputation may be damaged if someone makes a fool of himself or herself and appears to be incompetent or stupid. How many times have children been screamed at and told, "You're an idiot." As a substitute, yet with no less damaging impact, is the message of a cold, indignant stare that often penetrates right to the core of some youngster's opinion of self. As the personal opinion erodes because of lack of sensitivity on the part of another, self-esteem crumbles, ushering in the next line of defense, which becomes that old nemesis, unhealthy control.

The constant need to look good in every situation begins to take precedence over one's knowledge that he or she can adequately withstand the pain and pressure of rejection. This is where the anger comes in. Anger at oneself arises when our deepest truth is being rejected. The truth of human nature is this: each of us **can** handle the voice or look of rejection from both inside and outside ourselves in any given moment. We as humans know this and yet pretend as though it isn't true. The ambivalence felt within causes a disparity, which is the source of internal anger. This anger is created because of an outside situation where we are "not getting our way." We want justification. We are mad and ready to point fingers, scream at the irreverence of others for not meeting our demands, or intimidate by throwing our power around. Some, like those who prefer the silent treatment, enjoy using guilt as a means of controlling.

I always encourage my clients to do one thing in the midst of anger--stay focused on the awareness of it. It is my observation that anger will slowly subside if we give it permission to be there, in a place of prominence, until we cool down. The most important decision in the throes of anger is to give ourselves permission to observe it without judgment or condemnation. The observation process itself can often be a very humbling experience because we instantly notice the justifying thoughts that want to substantiate the continuation of the negative emotional display. Yet deep inside, each of us knows the lie. If we stop long enough to register that this wild, emotional extravaganza is nothing more than a **pretend** part of ourselves, we start to take back control over its power to affect important decision-making. Decisions based on anger are invariably contrary to our higher nature; therefore, they serve little purpose on the spiritual journey. Remember; give yourself permission to feel these negative emotional displays. Second, notice the justifiers that start popping up in your thought patterns. Third, pay attention to how far your anger-based decisions are taking you from your truth. Fourth, find the courage to stay with this process until you start to cool down. And fifth, notice the *lack* of power and energy you feel when making anger your chief motivator.

Most anger can be avoided by welcoming the future instead of dreading it, knowing how powerful we are in any given moment, raising self-esteem, and choosing to access memories of past successes when we've risked and succeeded despite our fears. As previously stated, once the truth of anger is revealed we have no legitimate excuse to use it as a destructive force. We therefore can work towards recognizing poor applications and prevent them from taking over future decision-making activities. Anger, in its simplicity, represents distraction. There is nothing more aggravating and inappropriate than to have anger as the key ingredient in decision-making. If this happens, it starts a loveless chain reaction, which ultimately will need to be addressed. The sooner we recognize a negative display of emotion and eliminate it from the decision-making process, the more spiritually accurate we become.

The easiest way to recognize the potential for a positive future is to accept the present. If you look closely at your life, you'll usually find out how successfully you've moved through adversity, hardship, loss and pain. Have you suffered a great loss? And now, being on the other side of it, are you still alive and continuing your day-to-day life experience? The answer to this question by most of us would be in the affirmative. Have you lived through suffering, loss, and pain? If the answer is "yes" then you have a proven track record. Wake up and realize that you're not as delicate as you may think. Your life is living proof of your resilience.

Ralph is angry because he does not know how to face his strong-willed wife. She can be demanding and very opinionated. Most of the time she can be defined as assertive, focused, and a powerhouse. Some of this man's anger has turned inward in the form of resentment. Some of it has turned outward in the form of distance. Ralph claims and shows a lack of interest, especially romantic passion, towards his wife. During our consultation I informed him that his subconscious thinking contained this fearful thought: "You are afraid that your wife will leave you; therefore, you keep retreating from her loving arms." He was in shock and dismay at my spiritual insight. I assured him, "Your vibrations are leaning in this direction." As we explored his present and past patterns, it became more apparent to him that I might be accurate.

This man's deepest anger is at himself for not believing that he can withstand the loss of his beautiful wife Wanda. His internal control issues are outwardly displayed in the form of impotency, the perfect justification for maintaining physical distance. Ralph had a steady stream of girlfriends before marriage, and he confided in me that each time he would get close to a relationship of any significance, which required the "giving of his heart," he immediately backed off and withdrew. He fears being left by Wanda and facing the aftermath--his internal judgment--which could easily label him a loser. Ralph also fears the reality of aloneness. He's grown accustomed to someone being around to affirm him, protect him and share life's treasures with him.

A central belief in Ralph's subconscious mind reads like this: "Use anger as a means of avoiding change because change could mean the possibility of permanent loss. You may never find another woman like this one; keep her at all costs." Unfortunately the cost can rob an individual of his health, mental stability, or focus on life's purpose. We begin to see the paradoxical nature of this man's life. On the one hand, he wants to leave out of fear because she may leave him first, thus creating devastating consequences. On the other hand, he fears leaving because of the potential loss factor, which would surely ensue. He has created a no-win situation for his life. As stated, Ralph's ultimate anger is at himself for being a coward. His tension and anxiety are rising, he is frustrated in his sexual life, and he is blinded by his own ego and sees no positive end in sight.

My suggestion to Ralph was simple, and because it has been applied with positive results in similar situations, I knew it could work. "Channel your creative passion in the direction of an appropriate outlet." How can this one simple suggestion be so effective? Each of us is here to *do good work*. The art of living effectively entails the activation of our creative spirit. If we do not honor and awaken this spirit on a continual basis, we become dull, dry, and withdrawn. Practicing the art of effective living is *doing good work* because one engages his or her purpose and shares his or her talents. The highest form of creativity and the greatest degree of satisfaction for Ralph come about when he chooses to stay tuned to his purpose. This man came in his present life form to teach music. When he is sharing music theory, composition techniques, or the simple art of teaching someone to read music, his spirit comes alive; thus he channels creative energy *in the direction of an appropriate outlet.* This simple shift in perspective is so validating and uplifting that it often takes the pressure off performance in other areas of life, especially sexual.

Anger dissipates when an individual chooses to create. A life of service, which involves servicing one's purpose as well as serving the world, is the job of every human being. When purpose is at the forefront of our attention we find the courage to move away from fear of loss, rejection, or ego demands in order to move creatively towards that main purpose. Psychology says, "Serve yourself;" spirituality says, "When you serve your purpose you automatically take in the welfare and highest and best interest of the human self." By deciding to create a life according to purpose, anger minimizes because decisions like Ralph's never surface. Anger comes about when we are caught between diametrically opposing forces, each attempting to pull us in a different direction. Ralph is afraid to go as much as he is afraid to stay. If he chose to walk in *spirit,* he would create paths, directions and goals for his life as easily as he could create music. Attention to the spiritual path insures appropriate outlets for our energy **at all times**.

Every time an angry thought takes over, compelling and beckoning you to make decisions because of it, ask yourself one simple question, "What does *my spirit* choose regarding my direction right now?" Immediately put that answer aside, take a deep breath, release the air from your lungs slowly, and ask again with deeper conviction, "What does *my spirit* choose for me right now?" Dismiss this answer lovingly, repeat the breath work, and the third time, with full internal conviction say these words, "What does *my spirit* choose that I create right now?" Most likely the third answer will bypass your ego demands, your psychological cravings, your fear and anger, and provide you with a most spiritually appropriate answer. The serving of the self and the attention to your Self have been rendered with the inclusion of one major theme: your creative passion and ultimate purpose have been taken into consideration in the process.

Anger comes when this belief arises: "I have no choice." The moment Ralph realized that he was in the driver's seat and activated his Spirit, he was able to discern and confidence began to resurface. For each of us the same phenomenon can take place. Choice is our birthright; choice is the gift of free will, and free will is a spiritual matter. This man gained confidence in himself because the practice of this exercise showed him that he was never alone. Spirit is always at his side and courage always resides within him to make choices no matter how unbearable he might perceive the results. Ralph now makes choices; he does not always hear the voice of truth showing him the way, yet he follows the exercise faithfully knowing that every day he gains more and more accuracy and life-giving courage.

I recently had an encounter with a woman that left me no alternative but to practice this exercise again and again. It was either practice or forsake everything I knew about the spiritual path and its exercises. The story goes like this.

I share office personnel with my partner. A temp had been hired to handle some of the filing overload. She was also given the responsibility of answering the phone and making appointments when the regular staff was busy. I received a couple of notifications from clients that their calls were immediately being rerouted to a regular staff person by someone who seemed very disinterested in helping them. She barely acknowledged that these people had indeed reached the right number. My clients were annoyed that this lack of immediate attention often caused delays in receiving appointments. After bringing up my dilemma, the temporary employee's explanation was this: "I do not believe in your work as a spiritual counselor. It is against my religious beliefs, and I will not make your appointments nor have anything to do with your clientele." Immediately the hair on the back of my neck stood up and a sense of outrage enveloped my mind. All I could think about was her inability to accept my path as well as her inability to resign once she had determined a conflict of interest had arisen.

Everything inside of my lower self was looking for ways to fault her, blame her, or put her down.

I felt myself becoming defensive and wanting to set her straight. I wanted to let her know the merits of my work and tell her what she was doing was *wrong*. All of these persuasions of the mind are entrapments, and I knew if I continued along this line of thinking, I would revert to old, negative patterns of interaction. I suddenly caught myself even though the ego was demanding that I take negative action. I found the courage to ask, "What does my *spirit* choose regarding my direction right now?" The first answer in the chain was "Get even." This made me chuckle and suddenly break the spell of anger. This then allowed me to ask in a more sincere way, "What does my *spirit* choose for me right now?" All I heard from the inner dialogue was "Open up more." A greater sense of calm started to wash over me, my anxiety diminished, and I was ready to ask the third time from a place of **all** sincerity, "What does my spirit choose regarding my direction right now?" In a flash of insight I knew; the ego's strangulation hold was loosened, and my mind was again free to come from a place of love. I was told by my Higher Self, in no uncertain terms, "Be the example of love in action, look at her not from a place of condemnation but from one of acceptance, and above all listen to her. She is at a perfect place on her path."

I immediately wanted to dismiss these words of truth and go on being angry at her; in fact, it took a couple of days in order to follow these words of truth because my need to justify, set her straight and make her approve of me would not let up. I had to go through this exercise many, many times in order to find peace and ultimate acceptance.

Chapter Six

Pain

"The harder the conflict, the more glorious the triumph."

-Thomas Paine

The spiritual nature of pain is simple; the physical and mental nature of pain is complex. In the midst of feeling pain we automatically turn to the mental, looking for ways to immediately create answers concerning relief. When approaching pain from the physical, the learned line of defense is to seek something outside of us to alleviate the situation. Spirituality would show us that pain is a messenger; it has a life and an intelligence of its own, yet it is intrinsically tied to the rest of our body-mind connection. The message of pain, when approached mentally, often leads to frustration. The first order of defense is, "I don't deserve this; this isn't fair." This kind of defense only exacerbates the problem because the true message is completely ignored. Similar results occur when the physical message of pain concentrates only on relief. Lessening an eventual elimination of pain occurs when the message is registered wholeheartedly within our consciousness.

The primary message of pain deals with imbalance. Anxiety, mental tension, or emotional stresses are clear indicators of mental imbalance. The individual who chooses a formula of logic and reason as the sole means of making decisions often suffers from the symptoms. The same symptoms will occur in the individual who relies on negative or runaway emotions to postulate answers to pressing questions. The imbalance comes when an oversimplified formula to problem solving occurs. Problems are never solved; *they simply eliminate themselves.* This occurs when choice is recognized as a personal right. Choices made when there is an imbalance between the heart and head increase the possibility of being stuck in single-mindedness. The mind, which believes it can only choose from a prearranged, logical formula or one prompted from a highly charged, negative, emotional cause, is imbalanced because thought is overly steeped in one formula. A blend of internal persuasions is always necessary if spirituality is to play a part in decision making.

When over-concentration on a nonessential definition or identity of who we are takes place, pain erupts. In our society the emphasis is on grooming our youth to become well oiled thinking machines. The belief emphasizes that if one thinks well, the avoidance of pitfalls in life will take place. The avoidance of pitfalls only takes place if one strives to move out of self-importance. The healthiest substitute for self-importance is self-realization. The realization always includes one's talent and purpose. The mind that strives to follow a prescription for life is always taxed. Strain ensues because a war takes place between what we are designed to be and do versus what the mind believes is important that we be and do. The mind believes because we program it to define us a certain way. This includes all limiting thought about our potential that is programmed into us during our lifetime. We fail to venture into activities that would promote our real purpose and talent which often leads us to be drained and debilitated. The mind holds on to non-essential data at any cost then uses it to jeopardize the welfare and safety of our bodies.

Eddie suffers. His suffering has driven him to seek out medical specialists as well as alternative therapies. I have reminded him throughout the course of our counseling that the cure lies in healing. This is very confusing to many of us because the elimination of pain by arriving at a cure seems to be the most important issue when it comes to answering its call. The message is stronger than the pain. The message asks that we move always in the direction of healing. **Healing takes place when balance has been restored**. Balance comes about by listening to the heart, honoring its direction no matter how weird or impractical it may sound, and finding the courage to use the miraculous ordering power of the mind to follow implicitly the directions registered.

Eddie's healing will take place when he decides to follow the main spiritual dictate concerning the concept of self. He is learning "to thine own self be true." If we analyze this dictate we're dealing with two main ingredients, "own self" and "true." The own self, in essence, is the Spiritual Self. Under this umbrella is our spirit, soul, life force, and purpose. These ingredients must always be substituted for self-importance and self-definition. If we try to create or manufacture these definitions, we will always come up short. Pain is the result of this attempt. Our true definitions and importance are unlimited, and because we think in limited terms, it is incomprehensible to fathom the extent of them. It is best for us to focus, if we are to maintain healing, on unlimited potential. Within this new, expanded, unlimited version of Self, freedom is remembered.

Being true to oneself means honoring specific tendencies and talents that are natural to us. The tendency to move towards a particular person, place, or thing is natural for human beings. If the mind has constructed limited concepts of where it should venture, constriction takes place; i.e., pain. My client decided a long time ago, around the age of four, to follow what others deemed appropriate, mannerly and safe. He left his natural tendencies behind, succumbing to the whims of society, which would soon become his adviser and chief decision-maker. Eddie sold out because of fear of ridicule and pain. Did he escape either one of these? Of course he did not. He has not won the favor of those he would like to impress, nor has he avoided pain.

Eddie's talent is in the field of consolation. He knows how to relate empathetically to others by connecting to their pain and suffering. His life of pain has created a natural bridge between himself and those he ministers to. He has learned the heart of support because he understands the nature of his fellow human beings. The lesson, being learned, can now subside. For Eddie to return to a state of pain free existence, he must let himself be led to the place where his talents can be most utilized. I encouraged this young man to remember what he enjoyed doing as a child. I encouraged him to look around, at every opportunity, and observe clearly from a place of openness what people, places and things he is interested in. Our natural tendencies and talents are no mystery if we observe this scheme of our lives. Our patterns clearly indicate what we most gravitate towards and hide from. Unfortunately, oftentimes what we gravitate towards most comes from society's dictates and not from our own natural tendencies. Our job, as is Eddie's, is to sort out the "small self" from the Spirit Self.

Connie wants to move--not only to a new geographical location, but also in directions that decrease her fears. Pain often materializes when there is an indwelling focus on what is not, as opposed to what is, inside a person's makeup. This woman wants security in her old age; therefore, she toils with a job that includes, as far as her perception is concerned, discrimination, poor attitude, unasked for reassignments, and inadequate compensation. She stays because her job offers her benefits that include a retirement package and health care. Security is important to all of us; false security threatens us. Stress is often an indicator that we have over-emphasized our need to use force to control the events of our lives. Control, in the form of structured attention and focus, is beneficial. Structure that prevents adventure from taking place is a false safeguard built upon fear of the unknown. We are put on this earth to explore so that ultimately we use our talents where they are most needed.

Connie's claim was that she could not afford to explore life because she was getting older and her stamina was waning. She, like many of us, looks for safeguards outside her own spirit nature to ensure that she is taken care of in her old age. I shared with Connie that the most important security is in knowing that stress subsides when we are engaged in activity that we love or know in our hearts makes a contribution to life. This kind of giving to our Self, by being willing to engage in activity that stimulates us, and of giving to others, by sharing the wealth of our talent with them, keeps us young at heart, physically fit, and mentally alert.

This spiritual shift is made possible only by conscious effort. Being conscious of what we fear is the first clue in understanding what path we are on. Connie's path was one of safeguard, and the more force she used to ensure her safety, the weaker and more depressed she became. I asked her to review her life from a standpoint of her own track record. Have you always maintained your financial security? Her retort was in an immediate, "yes." My job in this moment was to point out how impeccable her internal discipline really was. By taking a moment to review that, as an adult, she'd never been without work and had always maintained financial independence, she was able to laugh at her fear. From a standpoint of reality she had never let herself down, so why did she need to maintain her fear in the first place?

When we are led by runaway negative emotional data, fear is a predictable outcome. False feelings of lack of security envelop us. Connie was following this course instead of taking a moment to reflect upon her own performance record. It was impeccable, yet she still disregarded it in favor of some outdated subconscious program. Her mother had died leaving her and her sister orphaned. As a young child she only knew that she needed security and she needed it from others. As she grew older the realization that others could and would let her down became apparent. This built a strong need for independence and left an indelible imprint, which indicated the possibility of betrayal at any moment. The security of a loving, providing mother was snatched from her at the moment of her mother's death. Her subconscious program encouraged her to refrain from trust and used fear, prompted by loss, as its tool of motivation.

Loss of her mother helped prove that Connie could come to her own rescue and give herself provision in life. The downside of this experience created a stream of fear, which encouraged her to always cut her losses through minimal chance taking. Her decision to stay put geographically was a direct result of her need to cut her losses. This directive came to her as a child, prompted by the loss of her mother. Connie, like all of us, has a choice to make when faced with the possibility of a painful situation: stay put and suffer the consequences, or try adventure and prove to ourselves that we can overcome the emotional impact in case we make a poor choice. Many of my clients never get to that place of making a choice. Their physical pain is so debilitating to them that they are incapable of mobility.

Eddie's pain was so debilitating he could no longer lift himself out of the bed. His neck and shoulder would spasm rendering him virtually helpless. Pain so severe, throbbing relentlessly in his neck, caused him deep despair. Eddie's small self convinced him to create separation from the rest of the world by choosing to be overly critical. He was overly critical of other people's manners, choices, performance, style, courtesies and lifestyles. He wanted conformity and could become demanding when others were in noncompliance. At times he would include himself in his own condemning outlook but preferred to focus on his belief in the inadequacies of others.

Over time Eddie became open to the possibility that he had set in motion his painful existence. Of course, he did not will himself to be a man plagued with pain. His stubbornness to not reform and return to balance did provide fertile ground for ultimate discomfort. His discomfort took hold in his neck and shoulder. Even though his intention never was to promote pain in his body, he nevertheless set up the circumstances. The message his body was conveying sounded something like this: "You are miserable because you fail to accept what you aren't able to change. The stress over not getting your way will intensify until you give up the pursuit. Feel the pain of others, accept their efforts, honor their choices, and you will feel better."

Eddie's issue concerns his intense effort to change the things outside himself instead of focusing on what he can do to allow change within. A large portion of Western society agrees with Eddie. Each seeks to interfere with the paths of others, dictate what is right and wrong, or complain about what he or she has little or no control over. These endeavors camouflage the real work. Learning to love and accept the small self, despite its human imperfections, and learning to communicate with and trust the supernatural intelligence of the Higher Self are the most important endeavors we can accomplish. Eddie's need to blame is a substitute for introspection and his need to control takes the place of following the natural flow of life. Pain free minutes, hours and days ensue primarily because Eddie is in this state of remembering. He remembers more and more how to be unaffected and unattached.

A sure sign that we are living in a world affected by outside standards is when the word *should* is constantly flowing within a conversation. If you and I constantly ask anyone other than our Higher Selves what we *should do*, we are out of balance. Our early training taught us not to depend on our intuitive feelings but instead to depend upon maintaining the standards of society. This was a cruel joke primarily because these standards are constantly in the state of flux. Finding courage to ask our Higher Selves for direction is quite scary to most of us. We have been trained to consult the expert, forgetting that the expert is buried deep within yet is still accessible at our command. Using *should* always indicates that we are out of control spiritually.

The second way of knowing that you are out of touch and susceptible to pain centers on the need to be right. Being right is a very egotistical need proving that the ego's desires are in command. The ego's main purpose is to move us in the direction of sameness: same thought, action, or deed over and over again in cyclical fashion. Deciding that we are right fosters the ego's desires of perfection and control. It takes a lot of defense for us to be right because our main rebuttal is that someone else is wrong. Putting another down over and over again for their beliefs is a dangerous undertaking.

In this moment of audacity we're taking over the role of Creator, as some of our predecessors believed him to be. Most of our learning about the creative nature centers around a God who can spew out vengeance and disapproval when we have fallen from grace. The prophet Ezekiel warns that if I tell the wicked, "Oh wicked one, you shall surely die," and I did not speak out to dissuade the wicked from his way, then I shall die for his guilt. In this passage, God is ready to kill us if we don't chastise our brother. Maintaining the goal of being another's judge and jury is burdening. Eddie is burdened by his need to control life around himself by attempting to whip it into shape. He wants everyone to know the right path to follow and the penalty that he or she may incur if he or she is wrong. It takes a lot of time and attention to follow this track and it is a distraction from the pertinent issues of life.

And what are the pertinent issues of life? They are finding ways to restore peace and harmony to our countenance, engaging in activity that brings self-satisfaction, and serving the good of mankind by investigating and exercising our God-given talents.

Chapter Seven

Relationships

"We must learn to live together as brothers or perish together as fools."

-Martin Luther King, Jr.

Relationships define our place in life in a very realistic way. Every relationship has a projection aspect to it; we get to view our real selves in the lives of those around us. In our culture we've been taught to over-dramatize the permanence of relationships, often believing that they must remain intact and ongoing for us to be considered healthy by the psychological world. Changes in relationship can be a painless, joyful undertaking if we but apply the spiritual principles. Every relationship in one's life denotes a measure of acceptance for the personality, talents, or mannerisms of another. Relationships also show where our resentments lie regarding irresponsibility, unhealthy display of emotion, or lack of good judgment in the life of another. We grow little without a healthy dose of relationship in our lives every day.

The spiritual path shows us that attachments are our downfall and attachments to relationships are no exception to this rule. Culturally, we've been taught to cling to relationships because of the investment aspect. We invest time, energy, and focus on another, expecting like energy in return. It is easy to get caught in the trap of expecting another to perform for us, and we're taught to feel sad if someone leaves our lives before they've had time to do so. This expectation is a major source of discomfort for my clients with relationship issues.

The fatal flaw, after detecting what is undesirable in a mate, is to think that we can change him or her. What we can do is recognize our own flaw being so vividly displayed by the other party and seek to bring happiness back into our lives. *Staying in a relationship after receiving its lesson can be the most unspiritual act we will ever commit.* I've watched lives in torment; I've watched people suffer in disgrace, and I have seen the human spirit broken all because the emphasis was on changing another instead of changing one's self and one's circumstances.

Marcia claims that Bill is over-controlling, failing to listen, and constantly masking his feelings. She wants the man who was so willing to be tender and compassionate during their courtship days to return as the understanding yet strong knight in shining armor. Since Bill is not my client, I had not heard his side of the story, but from the complaints about her mate, it is obvious that Marcia is projecting on him what she refuses to look at in herself. Has Bill changed? After the infatuation process, where preferences are surrendered easily, one returns to old patterns of behavior and attitude. Knowing that each of us returns to our originality is why so many therapists encourage their clients to enter a long, observing courtship before serious commitment is to be considered. Marcia needs to examine every complaint and criticism she lodges against her mate because her lesson is to honor and change areas where she mimics his unattractive and undesirable behavior.

We certainly can't let Bill off the hook in the scenario, for he needs to maintain an open heart and plenty of understanding if he is to spiritually contribute to the relationship. Men are programmed to solve problems and fix things now. Despite this they are fully capable of accepting the unknown timetables of progress, which often feel like trials and tribulations to them. Bill needs to forego any internal timetable that he has concocted for Marcia's progress. It would be smart for him to revel, without jealousy, in the successes of his partner. Bill needs to remember that if he was open, caring, and feeling during the courtship process, he is certainly capable of continuing this experience long after his "conquest."

The biggest question I'm asked as the spiritual adviser concerns timing. Whether the relationship is with one's work, self or a romantic partner, knowing internally when to let go and move on is crucial. Marcia has forgotten to pay attention to her body signs as well as feelings created by *her Spirit*.

Often the relationship we have with work is so intertwined with our self-esteem that we overestimate its importance. Such is the case of Wanda. Her hair is falling out and her skin is dry and scaly. Her question, of course, was "why?" I immediately sensed that it had to do with tensions and anxiety caused by the need for outside approval. Wanda had started the conversation by describing herself as "dead in the water." I informed her that words could often be the prelude to a self-fulfilling prophecy. "Could your hair and skin's dying at such an excessive rate be an indicator that some part of you is listening to your words?" Body signs are always proof positive that we are out of sync with our *Spirit* selves and our soul's intentions for us. This woman is highly talented and creative. When she receives rave reviews for her work there is momentary contentment; when she is alone, the anxiety over not being good enough creeps into the silence.

The spiritual healing for Wanda will take place when feelings of security and self-accomplishment return. As an exercise, I encouraged her to stare into the dark, imagining that she is the only one left on earth to perform for. From this vantage point she could feel a sigh of relief and a loving pride in her work. All of the love feelings reside within us on a permanent basis, including self-approval, self-contentment, and self-understanding. Constant focus on our positive, approving nature allows us to get through periods of negative self-chatter.

Our minds often become reminders of our failure, thus prompting discontent with our present and future conditions. To stop this cycle means we can objectively focus on our deepest, most spiritual feelings, which guide us with love and deep understanding. Concurrently, we can honor internal creativity to the extent of inventing choices, which often prompts us to focus on new relationships in the world around us.

What are the signs that a relationship has run its course? Usually there is a nagging feeling of unrest and discontent, which seems to have no specific cause. Coupled with this internal dissatisfaction is the need to move forward, yet the path might be completely obscure to our rational, thinking minds. There is always mystery to this inner prompting, yet when it is there on a continual basis, trusting its message is always spiritual. I have advised hundreds of clients to remain steadfast when the opposite is true. The opposite of an internal discernment is always a demand from the ego. Instead of an internal knowing, what comes to mind is the need to escape. The justifier is always the same. "I'm being treated poorly and I don't have to put up with this crap." This is an excuse based on fear and has nothing to do with an internal prompting, which needs no negative justification. Running away never resolves the issue; it only prolongs the pain and prevents the healing.

If "I'm being treated poorly," it is up to me to take action, and the best course of action to take is to practice fearlessness. Poor treatment is a state of mind, yet your rebuttal to this might be, "If a woman is being physically as well as psychologically abused three times a day, isn't that more than a state of mind?" On a strictly physical level the answer is "yes." From the level of creation, the answer lies in the realization that we create our reality, so spiritually the answer is "no."

While in the employment of Catholic Social Services, I was assigned to work as a group facilitator for battered and abused women who were being temporary housed in one of our shelters. Their level of sophistication concerning the type and degree of abuse amazed me. As stories were traded each week, this became apparent to me; many of the women so cloaked themselves in abuse and its aftermath that they became their main source of identity. They cultivated the art of identifying themselves with abuse to such a degree that most could not differentiate between the experience of living sanely or insanely. I assure you these women were living insanely, almost inhumanely, and they had every kind of scar imaginable to prove it. It is absolutely true that abuse experienced in the physical is real; it hurts to the point of anesthetization, which is an almost impossible task to reverse.

If thought precedes form, which I am convinced it does, then it was the mind-set of these women that attracted "their man." He didn't just happen to stumble into their lives; he was ordered. Most likely everyone in the group had a father, or uncle, or even someone she may have befriended next door who coerced this innocent, beautiful child into feeling worthless, helpless, and unlovable. I saw the ingrained beliefs of sheltered women who were totally entrapped by their minds. They were still holding onto the opinions of others long after reaching a state of adulthood.

I will never forget watching an interview with Tina Turner which addressed the issue of living for almost twenty years with an abusive spouse. Ike Turner, according to Tina, could become explosive in a split second. She recounted eating chocolate one evening while riding in the backseat of a limousine with her husband. In a flash he started screaming at her to put the candy down because she might drop some and soil her dazzling white outfit. She recounted that in that moment something clicked inside of her--perhaps a glimpse of golden innocence-- and for the first time in her life, she had the strength to choose freedom no matter what the price. The ensuing battle--the first one she'd ever encountered with him because she always refused to fight back--left her battered and bruised and yet internally victorious for she had found a lost treasure, **fearlessness.** Tina could no longer go back; she knew that despite the risk she must return herself and her children to sanity. She recounted that she walked out of their hotel room after he passed out from alcohol and a drug-induced stupor and never, ever went back to him again. Tina Turner's reinforcement became Buddhism, which reinforced a need to accept responsibility for herself. She dedicated her life to being a peacemaker and found the ultimate reward of fearlessness, which to her was peace of mind.

Poor treatment is a mindset brought into physical reality because the person receiving it subconsciously believes that it is what he or she deserves. If my client were to run away and start anew, it would not be long before he or she attracts the same kind of behavior in his or her next partner. The answer lies not in escape but in creation. Creating worthiness to deserve loving treatment highlighted by respect, consideration, and understanding, is the real change each client needs to make. When the worthiness level increases to a point where self-love is the norm, the choice to leave unhealthy relationships becomes fearless, natural, and easy.

We can look from a different perspective at putting up with someone's "crap." Most of us have forgotten the lost art of being in a situation but not ruled by it. In this formula we are no longer giving another person permission to determine how we choose to feel. We take back our power and realize that we can be in the midst of even the most uncomplimentary remarks, inflammatory accusations, or intense criticism and still remain unaffected. Being in this state is the measure of true fearlessness. "Crap," at this point, becomes nothing but the outpouring of negative energy that is a signal of how dissatisfied the other really is with his or her performance in life. Oftentimes this person's main job is to try to bring us down to his or her level of personal betrayal and self hate.

The best time to leave any relationship is in that cathartic moment when we realize: "I can stay; I have the strength, but I really don't need or want to any longer. My heart is somewhere else. I feel it in the core of my being." Wanda was quick to point out to me, "My supervisor at work is a demon and she won't cut me any slack." My response was quick, "Cause and effect is the lesson you are learning. Leave because you want to, because there's opportunity elsewhere calling you, not because she's driving you crazy."

If the cause of our actions is outside ourselves because we fear the pain, loss, or inconvenience that others might bring, then the effect will always be low self-esteem and lack of self-respect. What others bring into our lives is simply energy. Wanda believed that another had the capability of determining her fate. In essence, she had decided this: "My supervisor is more important than I am and she has the power to determine my psychological well-being."

For Wanda, looking for a new job and changing her relationship with those with whom she came in contact at work would yield little in the form of relief. Wanda is her own demon and she won't cut herself any slack. Her life is fraught with discontent because of her looks, her weight and her inability to attract a romantic partner. She gets upset because the perfectionist in her demands that she do everything right or not do it at all. This capable woman believes that she has never found a fulfilling career because life has never given her the breaks she deserves. The list of goals in Wanda's mind that she should have accomplished by now in life, but hasn't, gets longer every year. Stopping this tragic downward spiral is simple, yet we often perceive it as a difficult undertaking.

The first act is to accept this truth: projection onto others is real. The second thing to do is examine all of the negative projections that we encounter each day. This can be reserved for reflection time, or better yet, done on the spot. Instead of being embroiled in another person's distasteful treatment of us, we should simply stop and say, "How interesting." The third thing to do is accept the demon in ourselves as an aspect of our active or repressed nature. This one admission is our ticket to freedom, for by accepting our potential to be a reenactment of the person whom we are so critical of, we free ourselves to enter forgiveness and learn better ways of behaving.

For Wanda, the demons are a product of her upbringing. Her spiritual nature demands nothing; it only requests that she accept her perfection instead of trying to achieve it falsely. The need to look acceptable in the eyes of society and work in a respectable place both come from outside influences. This young woman has forgotten that the best way to attract a loving, faithful partner is to be true to the job of loving yourself just the way you are with all your imagined flaws and imperfections. The double commands: "Make something of yourself" and "Don't be so stupid, you dummy," ring in the ears for years and often send mixed signals to young, impressionable minds. Self-confidence erodes every time a child hears, "No, no, didn't you hear me? I said, 'No.'" The creative spirit and internal knowing are substituted for the constant bombardment of debilitating messages from the outside world. If these self-destructive, confidence-eroding demands are shouted long and loud enough, we began to substitute belief in personal, innate wisdom for them.

With a little imagination and discipline, parents can learn to stop before the words, "No, no, no," start to come out of a their mouths to weaken their children's self confidence and increase the chances of permanent scars.

I believe that in certain instances of immediate need for safety the word *no* is perfectly acceptable and called for. When a little one is in the path of impending danger, it is hard to imagine using any other command. The rest of the time, which is a majority of the time, all parents are challenged to be spiritually creative when it comes to parenting. Take an extra moment if you are a parent, or are in a parenting role, and find in your consciousness the command you would actually like your son or daughter to follow. In actuality you want him or her to do something. "No" represents a standstill, stagnation, or shut down. It never represents positive action, which is what you really want in a situation. The inventive mind creates positive solutions so that you can avoid being a debilitating reinforcement in your child's upbringing and education.

As you can see, negative projections are often the continuation of one's upbringing long after he or she leaves home. The uncaring boyfriend and poor relationship with him become an extension of an earlier relationship with father. Marcia, the woman who felt abandoned because her boyfriend turned cold and unfeeling, continues to find men who lack the sensitivity and training to respond to her emotional needs. Her challenge is to cultivate the parenting ability within herself to provide nurturing acceptance of her own path and affirm her individual interests, style and abilities.

Wanda, who has abandoned her intuitive feelings and has forgotten to interpret her own body language, is realizing that the projection onto her body is a wake-up call. Finding the courage to follow her dreams can take the monkey of ill health off her back. Wanda associates the display of her creativity with recreation and needs to break from the voices within that encourage her to believe this. For her, a positive affirmation might be: "It is acceptable for me to be paid and paid handsomely for what I love to contribute to life." By doing this, which subsequently changes her belief, she will no longer need to punish her body for redefining the family's limited definition of work. It is obvious that Wanda was not affirmed for her looks and her physical capability as a child; therefore, she keeps finding supervisors who put down her skills and her personal way of accomplishing tasks. How long she keeps these childhood ghosts alive is up to her, yet the burden of keeping them ingrained in her subconscious thought is always heavy.

Leaving behind these imaginary relationships with parents, as well as projections they foster, can be a lifelong task for every adult, yet it is self-correction that we are all encouraged to create. Our higher selves are always delighted when we take this higher path of spiritual evolution. We are bathed in the light of truth each time we break out of old patterns and form relationships indicative of our beloved, creative natures. This can only be done when we honor and accept the highest use of projections, seek a loving relationship with our own creativity, and find the courage to change the things we're most afraid of changing.

Chapter Eight

Spiritual Partnerships

"I've learned that sometimes all a person needs is a hand to hold and a heart to understand."

-Andy Rooney

Relationships as we have previously known them, based on co-dependency, are slowly being phased out. The reason is simple: evolution of consciousness has reached the stage where the desire for two people to come together is built on a more solid foundation. Look at the divorce rate. Fifty percent of all new marriages end in divorce. The old rules don't work anymore. The commitments are spiritually unsound, and potential partners are unknowingly seeking ways to break old patterns.

Judy came to see me recently, wanting to make sure that she was going to attract the man of her dreams. I asked her what values she wanted in a man. Her reply was simple: "I want a man with integrity, honesty, and fairness." Her description is not unlike millions of other women. The secret formula is always the same: "Do unto others as you would have them do unto you." So many young people today go into the experience of relationship with a very long list of what they want as opposed what they might be able to give. If I ask a client, "What could you give?" there is often a period of silence and then a short list of attributes that society condones. The focus on receiving far outweighs the need to give in the eyes of a large portion of the world today.

Spiritual partnerships are based on a mutual sharing of gifts and talents that are both natural and honorable. Besides the obvious good a partner can bring into the relationship, there is also a need to cultivate the little used and often ignored capabilities hidden within. In my conversation with Judy, I expressed another underlying current of desire: the needed components to experience wholeness are often expected from the person we are in relationship with. When this need is based on a false assumption that we contain none of the attributes so easily identified within our beloved, then over-reliance on this person sets in. This is often termed codependency in psychological circles.

From a spiritual perspective, the major disagreement within ourselves comes when we fail to recognize what drives us. Our bodies, minds, and emotions are limited; our Spirit is forever and has constant access to the All Knowing. The over-reliance on someone else's talents stems from lack of recognition of one's own spiritual makeup. Spiritual partners are mentally clear about this fact and can quite easily detect motives for togetherness that are either life enhancing (spiritual) or codependent (fearful). If the motive for using someone else's capability is fear, ignorance, or laziness, then work at self-correction is needed. Each of us forgets that we have partners in the school of life to experience lessons with and learn from and that interaction with others is always a great gift.

The old paradigm of personal relationships states: "We are to expect a lot from our partner, complain if we don't receive, and feel used and victimized if our expectations are not met." These patterns, so contrary to spiritual law, have been around for thousands of years and have been the excuse for countless forms of dishonor such as slavery, prejudice, or slander--in marriages as well as other types of relationships. I tried to explain to Judy that the patterns of old paradigms reside in her DNA as well as the collective unconscious world better known as Spirit. This woman is not only dealing with what she has learned in this lifetime, she also is faced with cultural impressions so deep they go back hundreds of generations. Today's participants in relationships are pioneers, for we now have the ability to break these generational cycles and remember how to create the highest and purest relationships between ourselves and a beloved.

Judy has the power to start asking herself every day, "What virtues do I want exhibited by my future partner?" She can make a list of the ten most virtuous qualities desired by her and then keep score regarding how many of these same virtues she extols every day. As Judy stays determined to be what she actively desires and expects from another, she moves from codependency to authenticity and healthy partnership.

The beauty of being in the midst of someone who has his or her act together and polished is that we have a positive role model readily available. Being confident in displaying our talent is a great way of gifting our partner. The secret of an authentic spiritual relationship is to lovingly and humbly model our style, virtues, talents and accomplishments. The more we can go about being a positive, loving example, the more we contribute to the spiritual growth and development of another.

Sometimes jealousy ensues. It ultimately arises because we are mad at ourselves for not putting forth the effort to excel as our partner has. After examining this jealousy, deciding to own it, and then working through it with patience and understanding, we can return to place of a gladness because we're in the company of one so talented.

Many years ago I watched as Rebecca floated with ease through couples' counseling. She was open and gregarious, always relating to the topic at hand without reservation. Ted, her live-in boyfriend, was extremely introverted, a trait that many mistakenly define as shyness. A classic introvert always measures life by comparing it first to his or her own worldview. This includes strengths, intelligence, and degree of previous exposure to the present experience. The introvert warms to a situation, feels comfortable and safe, the more he or she begins to open up and become a part of the group. I could easily empathize with Ted because my personality profile indicates extreme introversion as my main entry point in life. I can also relate to Rebecca because I love to teach, lecture and share when I am well versed in the subject matter and have something important to share.

Ted's jealousy became apparent early on. He wanted desperately to face life as effortlessly as he perceived Rebecca and others like her doing. Unconsciously Ted would cut off her sentences or answer them for her, always giving the impression that he knew exactly what she was going to say. Her annoyance peaked and she lashed out at him. He immediately withdrew by retreating into a shell instead of finding the courage to stay with the conversation. For many weeks after this episode, we worked on communication skills which allowed Ted to feel safe to express himself in more and more healthy ways. Instead of finishing Rebecca's sentences, he found the courage to create his own. His resentment of her outgoing ways subsided because he had learned constructive ways to find his own voice and speak it clearly.

Owning the problem is often a space where many get stuck. They start projecting their anger and resentment onto their partners because their personal expectations aren't being met. These bright, intelligent individuals forfeit their happiness out of fear of looking "bad" or being compared to their partners. The jealousy and resentment come from feelings of inferiority, which can often be traced back to early partnerships with parents and siblings, teachers or peers. Oftentimes clients have been so browbeaten and hurt in the process of developing that they give up. The frustration of being a quitter indicates a need to "get off the hook" and divert attention. The focus of the interaction then becomes jealousy because the pain of facing the real issue—that of giving up—becomes too great.

Spiritual partners recognize in themselves where they fail to denote a sane, healthy, spiritual approach toward the other's talents. Once this situation is brought to light, unhealthy expectations, as well as resentment over accomplishments of the other, can be addressed and dismissed. Partners coming from a place of higher consciousness precondition themselves to go beyond the ego's demand to create both separation and neediness; instead, they create an opening of the heart. Remember that jealousy is a unique form of separation. The heart is always saying: "Give, give to your beloved, trusting that he or she will recognize your gifts, honor them, and use them in his or her own daily walk." Students are always asking, "Why does the ego often demand separation and at the same time keep me in codependency and neediness?" I believe the answer will always remain a mystery. My speculation is that it is a tool of Creator to remind us of our main purposes in life. To be successful with any relationship, including the one with ourselves, we must halt the belief in separation. Separation from a spiritual perspective means two things: we are created unequal and we are not of the same material as the Divine Source.

Separation always indicates a type of elitism that spirituality encourages us to eliminate. Our egos like to use the distinction between bodies, minds and sets of emotions as indicators that we should hold ourselves apart from others. If they lack and we have, we are to consider ourselves advantaged. If the opposite is true, we embrace the definition of an outcast, feeling inferior in the presence of someone who appears to have more. We play this game all day long, with the possibility of being seduced by it, with every new situation, even among our loved ones. If our mate has gained recognition in a special area, outwardly we may show signs of encouragement, yet inwardly we're dealing with a different attitude chosen by us towards our beloved. Over and over we concoct reasons to feel estranged, removed, or inept until eventually we solidify our belief in separation. Oftentimes those we are closest to are stand-ins for Creator. They become the outside influence that represents what God thinks of us and our performance in life. If we think we are created unequal, then we will go to every extreme to substantiate this belief, including setting others up as our gods and goddesses. Most of the time this is a subconscious act that we are unaware of until we start recognizing how easily we can overvalue another's opinions.

We are constantly working on person, internal partnerships, such as our relationship with our parents. Gloria inherited money from her father's estate including a trust for her daughter and herself. It was a sizable amount and under most circumstances one would be joyful to receive this most rewarding gift, but not Gloria. Amazingly she agonized in depth over how to handle her new fortune. All of her life this intelligent young woman had put more emphasis on what her father thought she should be than on her own regard for self. She still lived in the shadows of his example of how to handle finances. Just because he died, no magic wand was raised to eradicate this spell. Parental influence is perhaps the strongest captivation from which we must release ourselves. In our youth parents are exactly like gods and goddesses because of their protective ability. As children we would do almost anything to win their favor in order to avoid rejection, isolation, or lack of nurturing. In most cases our parents are our primary providers and we fear disturbing this delicate balance between them (safety) and ourselves (helplessness).

One of the most perfect moments in life is the split second we realize we no longer need our mothers and fathers. Contrary to the idea that it fosters separation, the break actually signals that we have joined the family of mankind and are ready to rely on resources that live beyond the veil-- such as Spirit communicating thought to humans to get its message across. By joining the family of mankind, our consciousness is aware of the bountiful resource contained in other human beings. We can receive nurturing, tenderness and compassion as well as motivation, direction, sound advice, and strong affirmation from a whole pantheon of human resources. This can include our friends, business associates, therapists, counselors, lovers, or even strangers on the street. The family of man is boundless when it comes to receiving affirmation from outside of us.

The Spirit realm is equally eager to offer support and guidance when we are feeling uncertain, unloved, or in distress. We each have personal guides who remain silent and noninvasive until the moment we invite their unfailing energy and information into our lives. Both these resources become the motivation which strengthens and enables us to give up the subconscious programs that keep us attached to our parents. Gloria did not want to keep living in the shadows of her father's way; she wanted to come from her own higher consciousness which is constantly in tune with the magnificence of the cosmic Father, Mother God. Once we are in tune with this force it will use every means available to get its message across.

Gloria now receives signals in the form of messages and actions from other human beings. She receives from the animal, plant and mineral kingdoms as well. Partnership with life is a sacred goal. Identifying the person who is willing to be a messenger in the form of example and/or as a spokesperson for Spirit is the goal. In conjunction, being open to the voice of nature is a completely separate partnership--one that requires special cultivation yet yields great rewards. Gloria's assignment was simple. Stay alert to anything that could be a message. Play with the information and look for any nugget of truth and inspiration from your spiritual partners. They are always present, always willing to assist.

Write down any particular events that might be insightful and contain cosmic wisdom. Share your messages with a trusted friend or spiritual teacher to get objective feedback. After discerning that you did indeed receive a spiritual insight, find the courage to take it to heart and implement it into daily life.

Chapter Nine

What Do I Deserve?

"One ought never to buy anything except with love. Anyone whatever, anything whatsoever, ought to belong to the person who loves it best."

-André Gide

Each of us deserves according to the way we view ourselves. If we are user-friendly towards our lives, then we can rest assured good things will be bestowed upon us. If we evaluate our performance in life as poor, then it is important to understand that we will attract very little useful substance to ourselves.

I have a particular client who never seems to be satisfied with his relationships. His family doesn't meet his expectations nor do his closest friends, nor does his sweetheart. This dilemma is like thousands of others I've encountered. To attract people who are friendly, considerate, trustworthy and kind, I encourage each of us who wants successful relationships to start taking two, important precautionary steps. The first concerns self-esteem. If I am lonely, it is because of the self-punishing factor. Because I don't feel worthy, those whom I would enjoy in my company slowly disappear. Self-esteem is often built upon repeated awareness of one's accomplishments. Every time any one of us succeeds in accomplishing a *loving* goal, it is important to document this fact. Keeping an accurate mental inventory of our accomplishments puts us in a more favorable light inside our own belief system. Each belief proclaiming we've done a good job at servicing the world or ourselves leads to the evolution of our positive self-evaluation.

Discernment is also necessary for anyone building self-esteem. Observing or witnessing ourselves being less than understanding, trustworthy or compassionate can lead to a sense of failure if we criticize ourselves long enough for the shortcomings. If we can observe our less than exemplary behavior without criticism, condemnation, or complaint, then we come closer to a state of spiritual discernment. Tacking negative feeling responses onto any conversation with ourselves over our performance immediately leads to lower self-esteem. In short, it is important to congratulate ourselves for jobs well done, evaluate ourselves objectively when we fall short of the mark, and never beat ourselves up mentally for a poor performance.

The second way to ensure that relationships of high quality flow our way is to put into action all the qualities we desire others to exemplify. My client Harry chooses to incessantly talk about the lack of response by others to his needs. The conversation quickly zeros in on his beloved Susie. In his mind she never becomes attentive to his hurting or longing which stem from painful experiences in life. He claims she is never there to console him. Harry's argument is always the same: "I want someone to be sensitive to my needs." My message is always the same: "If Susie fails to register or fulfill your needs, it's because you attracted her subconsciously long in advance of the present moment." This woman came into his life because she represents, in part, the punishment he chooses to bestow upon himself because of low self-esteem. I'm not claiming that he is consciously aware of his endeavor; I'm stating that on an internal level of **need** he has handpicked a woman incapable at present of intuitively or cognitively registering his discomfort and consoling him adequately. Susie is the manifestation of his own needs to punish himself. Because he thinks so poorly of himself, he is stuck in selfishness. Harry's selfishness leads him to serve only his ego drives. Consequently he has very little time or energy to tend to the hurts and pains of others, including his beloved who is doing the best she can with the background she inherited.

The dilemma of low self-esteem, coupled with a decision to refrain from giving unconditionally the behavior that he would like to receive, keeps Harry alienated from positive relationships. He will attract those people who mimic and represent his own dissatisfaction with life. Healthy change consequently centers on practicing the art of prevention. When any of us prevents our runaway ego from designing our negativity, we block the self-punishing factor. No longer will our negative evaluation block us from deserving all we're entitled to. As we practice being who we want others to be, we practice the law of giving and receiving. Spiritually speaking, we get back the energy and intelligence that we give out.

Harry also has to contend with the attachment factors of his life. An attachment to a predetermined outcome is a *runaway* desire. It is an obsessive thought that won't go away. One claims happiness contingent only upon the satisfaction of his or her obsessive longing. He constantly battles a subconscious belief that states: "If I give out anything, I **expect** a return on my investment." This belief is familiar to almost everyone on the planet. Here in the Western Hemisphere being cheated or deprived is considered a major tragedy. To prevent this from taking place, one common approach practiced is the art of intimidation or threat. This brief encounter with fear is supposed to bring the person who owes us to his or her knees and cause him or her to feel remorse. In actuality, it alienates all of us who try this technique from those we are trying to convince because it fosters an unhealthy, co-dependent relationship with the other party. This man's girlfriend is sick and tired of all the strings he puts on his giving. Susie is preconditioned to his ways and knows in advance that Harry will somehow ask for a favor in return for what appears to be a gift. This interplay creates tension within her because of the association factor. She associates his hidden agenda with every other man who has ever surprised her with manipulation and betrayal. Harry then wonders why she becomes withdrawn, sullen and suspicious of him.

At this point, I always encourage individuals to take responsibility for their lives. If Harry has attracted this drama, he has the power to dismiss it. Immediately within his grasp is the ability to decide to catch himself in the midst of the negative attachment. An attachment is always registered within us because of the anger factor. Anger is often an outward expression of fear. In this case it is fear based on wanting a predetermined outcome. We plan in advance the conclusion of our desires. As we dwell on this outcome and get upset over the possibility of failure, we reach a state of anxiety. As you can see, the experience is predicated on the fear of *not* getting our way and is often registered by a negative expression of anger.

Attachments are best dealt with by observing their influence on our bodies. Once registered we can start disassembling them by doing two important things. First, we can find out who the author *really* is. After some gentle soul searching, we often reach the startling conclusion that the original belief is not our own. Secondly, we can *own* the fear, anxiety, and anger that are created by not having our way. Owning a fear leads to its dissipation not its development. A fear envelops us when we try to pretend it is not there or is unimportant. Once we realize that "having our way" was not authored by us, we give the **need to fear** less importance. Realizing that we need not move in the direction of our false persuasion frees us to let go of the energy we put into pursuing it. At this point we usually dismiss the fear cycle and begin to ask ourselves the all-important question, "How can I give myself what I **really** need?"

As you can see, the art of cultivating high-level relationships begins with self. The ability to display in advance the attributes and values we would like to receive is an ongoing task. This, coupled with the art of loving ourselves while we are observing our negative behavior, is also a key factor in attracting healthy relationships. By doing this we eliminate the punishing factor of attracting those who make our lives miserable and unfulfilled. There is no need for attachment when all that we really want is at our fingertips.

The art of positive affirmation is one of the most beautiful gifts you can give yourself. Pursuing the art of negative affirmation leads to a disappointing, often difficult existence.

Each affirmation brings us closer to the realization that we are essentially Spirit. As Spirit we encourage ourselves to think in terms of love. Conversely, we can also think in terms of evil and destruction. Our spirit nature is ultimately one of peace and radiant joy, yet because of free will we can focus in any direction desired.

Every day, each time that an individual confirms his disappointment through condemnation, seeds of personal, often physical, destruction are planted. When an affirmation of positive value is repeated continuously throughout the day, it sets the stage for loving change. When the same affirmation contains enthusiasm, the image blossoms as a powerful tool. Each person's mind converts thought into an image. This image creates an overlay replacing old patterns in our minds. Subconscious programming controls these patterns and most of our decisions are formulated from them. In order to break a pattern, we need new images coupled with a directive, an affirmation.

Phillip came to me with health concerns. He wanted to change his eating habits. For most of us, eating is a repetitive experience. We learned at an early age to mimic the tastes of those around us. Research shows that left to our own devices, we would probably gravitate to foods that are good and nutritious for our body. Yet without the encouragement to trust the body's innate wisdom, most of us mimic the eating habits of our family.

To return to our natural instinctual way of choosing food, we must establish a concrete directive. I suggested to Phillip that he use three affirmations: "I am healthy," "I eat healthy," and "I drink healthy." At this point I asked him to remember a time in his life when he experienced optimum health. Phillip immediately captured an image of the day he purchased his first new automobile. In his mind's eye he pictured himself behind the wheel enjoying the freedom that only a top-down convertible brings. Phillip could feel the sun's warmth against his skin plus the freedom of the rushing air. In the brilliance of this event, he associated himself with perfect health. This recall, in vivid detail, of a young, healthy body elicited strong positive feelings, which are the perfect aid to any affirmation. Without a positive association, the likelihood of turning affirmation into victory diminishes proportionately. It is possible to achieve a goal through intellectual pursuit, such as repeating the affirmation over and over, yet it is more useful and timesaving to combine the mental with highly charged emotional input to enhance the process.

There are two distinct kinds of emotional input that energize the process of change. The first we shall call negative emotions. Each of us over a lifetime creates thousands of affirmations based on our association with them. Fear tops the list of negative emotions. Of course fear has a positive use in the world of every human being. We cannot function successfully without being afraid of certain physically harmful everyday situations. Ultimately the goal is for the fear to give way to awareness. A truly aware, spiritually awake individual will use love of life as a motivator to avoid harm.

Drinking a poisonous substance will kill us; therefore, to be afraid in the beginning is necessary to ensure our longevity. Healthy fear is always taken into consideration on the spiritual path, yet what happens to individuals in their early development can be considered no less than a national tragedy in contemporary society. Well-meaning parents and guardians endorse fearful affirmations and pass them on to their children out of ignorance and superstition. These budding beliefs once ingrained in the subconscious become the basis for major decision-making. Negative emotions, based on false assumption that a certain person, place or thing is harmful or dangerous, begin to set a damaging precedent. Fear, out of proportion with the reality of the situation, all too soon becomes the theme of young, impressionable minds.

My client could remain stagnant in his quest to eat healthy by using overly fear-based affirmations and motivation, or he could practice ones that may take longer yet ensure more long-term results. If Phillip encourages himself to eat better because he doesn't want to get fat, sick or die, he is operating from the assumption that food is bad or harmful, and he must refrain because indulgence in eating can be dangerous. This gross generalization is a lie and a ploy to control his eating. Certain foods can be eaten in volume without adverse effects. Intellectually most individuals know something about healthy nutrition, yet they put that knowledge aside when the taste buds scream for a certain food no matter what the fat, sugar, or caloric content. The average citizen has been exposed to enough information to have a rudimentary knowledge of what foods are healthy or not healthy to eat, as well as how much is enough without straining the body.

Phillip's old affirmation was "I can't eat that; it's bad for me." Most of us have a similar *line* which ultimately works to no avail. Fear of clogged arteries, cancer or a stroke usually goes out the window the minute that pungent, mouth-watering aromas waft the air. When the moment of temptation arrived, did Phillip honor his fear? According to his sad reports, it almost never happened. He had desensitized himself from his worst nightmare of poor health. His fear was no match for his love of highly desirable, yet unhealthy, foods. At this point I knew Phillip was ready for something new.

Week after week I would have him recall his spin in the convertible. That day many years earlier just happened to be his birthday, so he was extra jubilant. This image gave him a wonderful, positive undergirding for a new approach to change, far more useful than his old threatening, fear-based one. Over time his mind began to resonate with his Spirit, and a feeling of exuberance over the love of his body began to preside in his subconscious. Instead of using intimidation, threats, gilt and shame--all fear-based motives--he chose appreciation, loving dedication, and positive excitement as new motivation. These new reasons to eat healthy, drink healthy, and breathe healthy all support physical longevity so that he can enjoy the delights of life long into the future.

Life has constant enjoyment for those who move past fear. Part of Phillip's resistance to good health was tied to fears so ingrained and deep seated that even he didn't know they existed. He had so many fears that hadn't been desensitized through the process of spiritual evolution that he lived in constant fear that associates were out to get him in business or that women he opened up to would hurt him deeply. He feared being wrong and looking stupid, thus being judged harshly by his peers. Living under the strain of constant judgment always takes its toll on the physical body. Dissatisfaction with life creates eating problems, which are vain attempts to satisfy one's inner hunger.

The more Phillip chooses to uncover his hidden, mysterious culprits, the more he has to work on. The more he works on overcoming his deep-seated fears by reprogramming his mind through the interjection of positive affirmations, the easier it is to receive from the universe's great bounty. The formula for self-correction is simple, not only for Phillip but for all of us. As one of my great teachers, Dr. Giuseppe, once said, "There is no lack in your world; there is only a distribution problem." Each time we tap unique inner resources to create loving, deserving images of ourselves and ingrain them to our consciousness, we attract to us the useful things we want and deserve—all the good that life has to offer.

Chapter Ten

Preplanning Your Life

"Thinking always ahead, thinking always of trying to do more, brings a state of mind in which nothing seems impossible."

-Henry Ford

Is there a need to preplan one's life? The most logical reason to answer in the affirmative is this; *if we don't plan it someone else will.* That someone else lives within us as well as without. The someone within is the subconscious programmer that asks us to follow without question. The plan outside of us lies in the form of direction that we take without question from others. The prerequisite for all preplanning is to have our higher Self question ourselves concerning purpose, power, and motive. Spiritual planning can lead to following your truth in day-to-day activities. In essence, if you do not plan your day, it will be planned for you.

Your life, for the most part, is the product of your subconscious desires. Statistics show that more than ninety percent of our day-to-day decisions are subconsciously motivated. If you dislike how your life is being lived, question the source of your motivation. Fear, which lies just under the surface, is often the great motivator of the mind. Unfounded fear then becomes an unfounded belief when left unchecked. Observe what you hate the most, for it is a clue to some deep residing fear which has never been resolved.

Jackie hates hurting other people's feelings. She claims a need to be serving, altruistic, and loving. Her motive is this: "I always want to be loyal." My instructions to Jackie are simple: "Ask yourself every time a loyalty issues arises if you have the guts to be loyal to yourself." The real issue is that this woman hates herself for not following her deepest desires. When faced with choosing what she wants or choosing out of loyalty, she always takes the latter. A subconscious motivator, at this point, is planning life. Jackie seeks the easiest route possible because she fears the disapproval of others. If she "hurts their feelings" they might not like her anymore.

In my client's case, her day is ruled by other people's opinions. She plans according to the path of least resistance. For about the first thirty years of my life, I chose to live my life by this same criteria. "I will be good in their eyes so that they will give me the love and respect I deserve and desire."

By living life this way, signs of unhappiness with our decisions, or lack thereof, begin to emerge. A sense of low-grade agitation begins. If left unchecked this behavior will ultimately create depression and despair. The antidote for this condition is always the same: infuse courage into your belief system. I encouraged Jackie, just as I encouraged myself so many years ago, to wake up and repeat this simple affirmation: "I can do whatever it takes to live **my** life."

I prompted her to start planning now for the future. Jackie's stuckness, like that of so many other clients, revolved around a dysfunctional love relationship. Her subconscious program said, "I could never leave him." In reality she was choosing not to leave Mark because of the risk factor. She did not know in advance the reaction she would receive from this declaration. The assumption that he would act unfavorably was high, in fact, almost assured. Her subconscious program declared that she could not withstand the impact of Mark's disapproval. So no matter how incomplete her life was, her choices would not include the possibility of leaving this man.

Every day of Jackie's life is preordained to be lived in fear of the unknown. Each hour is filled with the belief that she might not survive emotionally the consequences of her actions. Millions of people, including myself, are capable of falling into these traps. The smart person observes his or her behavior and then asks the faithful question: "Is this how I want to live?" If the answer is "no," he or she considers this option: "Can I do whatever it takes to return myself to peace, harmony, balance, and sanity?" Oftentimes knowing conclusively in our heart of hearts that we have the wherewithal to do whatever it takes eliminates further testing.

Every dysfunctional interaction and relationship is a means of testing ourselves. If we preprogram our lives knowing that choice is an inherent right, things immediately start running smoother for us. The positive outcome of the decision to choose ushers in spiritual revelation, for in this moment the highest force that drives us, our Spirit, takes charge. Invincibility is felt and we return to a state of personal power. Risk in this supernatural moment becomes less and less frightening; the art of making choices because they feel right engulfs our senses.

Many wonder what the tests of life are all about and why we have to undergo them. This is an inappropriate description of what actually transpires. I like to think in terms of lessons to be learned. The lessons are those of **rightful living.**

Rightful living takes into account two things. First, we live in allegiance to the universal precepts, and secondly, we learn to listen and follow our true Spirit. The universal precepts start with one great fact: cause and effect reign without exception. Just as the physical law, so beautifully discovered by Newton, advocates that "every action has an equal and opposite reaction," so too does the Spirit world abide by this principle. Every time any of us forgets this law we, by our very makeup, nature and purpose, are prompted to remember the *truth* by experiencing a lesson. The focus of every lesson is always the same, a need to remember the truth. The content of the lesson varies according to our progress and our place in space and time.

Let's explore the background of Joe, a client whose mother has mastered the art of getting attention by attracting illness and disease. Spice this dysfunction with the use of intimidation, guilt, and fear as a means of motivating her children. It's no wonder that Joe has been dealing with a pain in his neck since the age of eleven. In his job he deals with abuse between parents and children. He also teaches anger management. This admirable young man, even though the outward conditions of his life have changed, is still dealing with subconscious programming as a primary directive. He gets attention in manners similar to his mother, especially by wanting others to pay attention to his physical ailments.

He finds it difficult to eliminate family patterns of guilt and intimidation to motivate the parents and their offspring whom he is instructed to teach every day. Joe's lessons are still in front of him moment by moment. His body is a war zone. Joe's pain is induced by stress because he fails to *live rightfully*. His true heart yearns for him to pay attention, yet he fails to listen. Joe is looking for the courage and ability to drum to his own beat. He yearns for a conviction of the heart which could prompt attention by accomplishment instead of aches and pains.

His neck pain is an indicator that life is "a pain in the neck." The consequences of using personal power at the risk of disappointing others is just too scary for this young man. Like mother, he activates the subconscious belief initiating negative emotions in order to make an impression on life around him. He has forgotten to preprogram himself to include love, understanding, and heartfelt emotion as a means of influencing others. This can include any art of discernment often defined as intuition, precognition, premonition, a sixth sense, gut-level feeling, spiritual insight, or inner knowing.

Joe was assigned to say this affirmation hundreds of times daily. "Life is good; I am complete and whole and I accept my powers to create my life." This affirmation, when taken seriously, frees Joe to remember who he is. By following it he can find the confidence to activate the true heart, which gives, knows, and follows the spiritual laws. The true heart always contains the highest level of feeling as opposed to emotions driven by the ego. It also accesses the "still, small voice within." The affirmation also reminds him that the wisdom to guide his every step lies within. Finding power gives him the confidence to become a follower of the Way which is perfect in each new moment.

Chapter Eleven

Say "Yes" to Life by Identifying Your Choices

"As human beings, we are endowed with freedom of choice, and we cannot shuffle off our responsibility upon the shoulders of God or nature. We must shoulder it ourselves. It is our responsibility."

-Arnold J. Toynbee

I was recently conversing with a client over the way he chose to confront his girlfriend when she decided to spend time with another man. After confirming his right to be angry and frustrated, I began to share with him the higher meaning of his experience with Gail. "You have given your power away," I kept saying. He could not relate to these words, so I explained to him what this phrase means spiritually. To give one's power away means simply this: permission is granted to another to determine your fate, which includes attitude, disposition or demeanor. Every time Danny says, "You hurt me so badly," he has forgotten who is in charge of his life. If Danny could have felt ownership of his life and his capability to call the shots, then he would have identified all his choices concerning the betrayal experience.

Our minds are trained to believe that others are responsible for what happens to us emotionally as well as physically. The truth, therefore, is often a mystery until we unravel it. We are so programmed to think of ourselves as only having *limited* choices, it is hard to fathom *unlimited* ones. The unlimited thinker embraces his power and this is what Danny refuses to comprehend.

Most of us are taught to think small. A perfect example is the flagrant misuse of "no." How many times a day do we hear this oftentimes useless word? For many it's hundreds, which shows a sign of cultural castration. One of the most uninspiring, unspiritual things we can do is think of responding to life's situations by saying "no." The limited concept and judgmental delivery of **no** is debilitating because it stifles the creative process. There is nothing more unimaginative than a harsh, barren, overly-exaggerated declaration of the word *no*. Danny is on the planet to create his life, not limit it or relegate it to a place of non-action. When he fails to declare a plan and say "yes" to it, he leaves Spirit out of the experience entirely. Our Spirit longs to soar and follow the creative process; **no** signifies an attempted destruction or block of this capability. Proclaiming **no** fails to offer an option or tell us what we can do in place of the perceived wrong.

Each time this talented, young man fails to recognize his capability and plummets into the trap of believing that someone else controls his destiny, he gives away his power, forgetting that it's the power to create that sustains one's life. Danny's rebuttal is always the same: "Gail acted in ways that were unbecoming, disheartening and rude." According to him, and culture, it may very well be that she acted in unethical ways. Yet the fact remains that each of us is in charge of determining the deleterious effect that another's actions have on us. I was quick to point out his lost perspective each time he demanded of her: "You can't talk to me this way anymore," or "Don't you dare knock on my door ever again." Every time we attack a person and then insist upon what he or she is **not** going to do to us, we have entered the world of illusion. Perspective has shifted from her choice into the trap of **no you can't.** The truth remains-- **yes she can**!

My job with Danny is to remind him, "Authenticity returns each time you share with another person, whom you believe has acted inappropriately, by stating your personal choices." Most of the time when fingers are pointed and accusations are made, it is a vain attempt to express one's deepest, most painful feelings. These don't always need to be shared with the person who acted without discretion or concern. It may have been more appropriate for Danny to find the courage to vent his disappointment with a trusted friend who would not have been affected by the full brunt of his fury.

Spirituality teaches us that all lessons have simple reasoning behind them. If someone keeps deceiving us by lying, cheating or falsifying the records, we first have an obligation to make better choices of companionship in the future. Secondly, we have to ask ourselves why we created the attraction of this person into our lives in the first place. Danny's girlfriend's betrayal was no accident. On some subconscious level he helped set the stage for this uncomplimentary event. His job is to search his higher intelligence until he understands the meaning of the attraction to someone who would act in a cruel, unbecoming way. Oftentimes through deep introspection, the projection reality surfaces, and we realize how much like the other person we are.

My job with all the people like Danny with whom I come in contact is to help them remember to take control of their lives, even in a situation of betrayal and anger. They can do this by constantly stating what they are going to do about their hurt and pain instead of needing the other person to mend his or her ways or change in a fashion demanded by the complainer. If each of us stays focused on choice, life becomes freer and more empowering. Verbalized, affirmative action is then substituted for finger pointing and unbecoming accusations.

At this point in our conversation Danny's reaction becomes very predictable. His burning question is always: "Who is going to punish Gail and set her straight if I don't?" I'm quick to inform anyone who asks: "The guilty one is quite capable of punishing him or herself and does so on a consistent basis." In this case, Gail not only receives instant punishment through Danny's scathing rebuttals and attacks, but she also continues to gravitate towards men who use and deceive her. She then punishes herself by claiming the victim role, thus feeling constantly sorry for the ill treatment she receives from the outside world. Her punishment is very real and self-perpetuating. Gail is a miserable woman who feels that life has passed her by.

What is Gail's role in this scenario? Whenever someone is critically judged, accused and told what to do, the most spiritual act that can follow is moving out of the energy of this abuse. A healthy critique of someone's performance is completely different from the fine art of blaming. Blaming is a limited, uncreative act. The Universe is constantly seeking solution through creative action, an example well worth emulating. The most important thing to do when someone is lodging a complaint against you is to observe his or her attitude. Gail's most important task concerning Danny's lashing out at her was to observe the presentation. If he had shared his frustration without pointing fingers and telling her what she should do, then I would have considered his act noble. At that point, Gail would have been wise to listen. If Danny had taken a more positive attitude and expressed his perceived needs, I would have considered him courageous, and so could she.

A most noble experience for Danny is finding the courage to share his inner feelings. If he just could have said, "I'm frustrated, tired, scared and hurting inside," then he would have acted truthfully. By saying to Gail, "I need honesty in our relationship and I'm willing to work at making it safe for us to communicate," he would have shown a great act of courage. When he moves from positive to negative judgment, he begins to camouflage the real issue, which is: "What can I do to create relief in my life?" A simple question with a simple solution--this is the spiritual way.

Whenever we return to the only place we have total control over, realignment with power begins. Gail stands in her power when she makes a conscious decision to be unaffected by someone else's attack. After determining that the attack was malicious, because Danny insisted upon sharing what she should do instead of stating what he needed to do, Gail would have been smart to catch her anxiety level rising. A high anxiety level is often a springboard towards the decision to "fight fire with fire." If only she could have remained cool, found a word or phrase to deflect his accusations and repeated it over and over until regaining composure, she would surely have followed a more spiritual path. I like to focus on two words when I'm in this position of being bombarded and potentially affected by another's energy. These words are "I'm cool." Repeating them after every negative comment slowly ushers me into a place of awareness. At this point I'm able to monitor my resistance, anxiety and building tension. I've noticed that when these three are raging I usually come from a place of uninspired intention because I've allowed my negative emotions to rule.

It is often considered difficult work to reverse the teachings of family and culture. More than one person would have encouraged either Danny and Gail to defend themselves, not put up with this garbage, or fight for their rights by constantly claiming that these directives are the formulas for staying in one's power. I believe they are the formulas for staying in one's own personal hell. Negative resistance is an excuse to hold onto grudges, and it alienates us from the party or parties we both fear and need to accept the most. What then is the alternative to an attack, which is often labeled the perfect way to fight back? The best defense is to become the offense, make a choice, create a plan of action, and stick to it in the most forthright way. Society overly emphasizes focusing on a negative defense as opposed to creating a healthy offense.

A woman whom I considered a friend once gave me a beautiful Native American-styled healing wand. Victoria was a gifted artist and had painstakingly handcrafted a most magnificent piece expressly for me. I enjoyed using this unique present in my work as well as keeping it on display in my office. Years later I received a phone call from this woman. Victoria stated that she would be by to pick up the wand because I was no longer, in her mind, justified to use it or have it in my possession. I had considered the gift mine and was put off by her conditional giving. My choice in this moment was to defend my territory, keep it at all costs--

which might include fighting for what was "mine"--or to turn over the wand lovingly, bless this woman and go about my business. I chose the latter; some might say my choice was out of cowardice, yet I believe it was practicing the art of detachment. My love for this instrument was real, and in order to know the depth of this reality, I was given a test. By defending my right to it, I would have displayed a weaker side to my personality so my plan of action was to love her, return the "gift," and bless her each time a negative thought about her arose. It was difficult in the beginning, but with perseverance my higher consciousness and higher capability won out. We are once again friends, and knowing her further enriches my life. By systematically letting go of this healing instrument, I believed I was honoring its true essence. By fighting I would have shown my lack of faith in the Universe to provide; by fighting I would have reduced myself to the same vibration that she was choosing to exhibit.

I've alluded often to the creation of human illusion, any belief that is contrary to spiritual law. Each of us can be a David Copperfield and make the truth disappear from our awareness. Even in the midst of extreme pain, presumably caused by another, we have the option and capability to switch perspectives back into higher consciousness and maintain awareness. In every situation we are in charge of our reaction; the illusion comes when we forget this simple truth.

When engaged in conversation where the subject matter is disagreeable, new to your belief system, or annoying in any way, consider these suggestions. Learn to be a good listener so that you win the admiration and confidence of your partner in conversation. Every time you notice your anxiety level rising and your need to interfere in the conversation, catch yourself. Start by making a conscious decision to return to listening, so that comprehension remains high and acceptance returns. Decide to save up your rebuttals for a time when it is your turn to have the floor. I would suggest it be a future time slot after you have assimilated and fully comprehended the other party's side. Every time apprehension starts to rise because you want to "get a point across," stop and say to yourself, "How interesting." This trigger will remind you to stay open, lovingly lower your apprehension and anxiety, and return to a focus on the subject at hand. This type of communication comes powerfully and positively from your heart.

If your conversational partner wants to badger you into an argument, you can reply in one of two ways: "I'll take your message under advisement and get back with you later," or "Let's talk about . . . ." This usually steers the conversation towards a less volatile subject matter. Your first thought might be: "This is avoidance." I do not consider this copping out for two reasons: Number 1) by recognizing your tolerance level you become your own hero; Number 2) if you are dealing with someone who is used to getting attention in negative ways, he or she will go to any extreme to get you to shower him or her with negativity. If a child grows up needing attention because of low self-esteem, he or she will often act in unflattering, unhealthy ways in order to receive it. This same child-like mentality can exist in a grown-up body, so don't assume you're dealing with maturity just because someone is of age.

When you decide to lead the conversation in productive ways, choosing to come from a place of power can be extremely rewarding. I always encourage a client, who wants to get a point across to his or her mate, friend, or acquaintance, to find out the deep interests and goals of the other person, ask for explanations, seek out the mechanics, or inquire about the starting point of the person's interests. This, coupled with sincere affirmation and a genuine desire to have the other succeed, helps establish equanimity and avoid the temptation of negative conversation.

Because you have shown interest in another, it sets the stage for him or her to be more open and receptive when it's your turn to share. The most important thing about sharing is this: make sure it comes from a place of action; never apologize for your dreams. Leave out any need to ask permission when stating your plans. Constantly act as if it is your decision and yours alone, yet kindly take into consideration the feelings, attitudes, and beliefs of the other party. If you find yourself asking, "Do you think I should do this or that?" remind yourself that you can just as easily say, "Here's what I'm thinking about doing. I would like to share my ideas with you and am open to feedback."

From this vantage point, you are no longer being the victim or asking another's permission to live *your* life. What you're doing is brainstorming with an audience of one, deciding in advance that you can handle any criticism while welcoming any helpful, sound advice. If your partner in conversation misconstrues your intentions, lovingly clarify that you are only **brainstorming** and are not asking him or her what you should do. Remind the person, lovingly, that you are stating your proposed intentions and any feelings that might have prompted or backed up these possible actions. By following this formula you're more likely to stay within your power, be appreciated for your forthrightness, and respected because you recognize who's in charge of whom.

Chapter Twelve

If You Can't Say Something Positive, Remain Silent

"Speak well of others and you need never whisper."

-Chinese Proverb

One of the easiest disciplines to accomplish from the standpoint of effort is the art of remaining positive. Constantly in the daily routine of life we're being asked to enter into the negative world of criticism, condemnation, and complaint. Many clients have asked, "Why does this temptation exist?" The answer, as in every other question concerning *why*, is this: because it is part of the gift of free will. Free choice is at the core of every single mental decision we humans make. The choice to follow love or its absence is an inalienable right, integral to the construction of our path, present in every moment of our lives.

The decision to share in the name of love is as easy as the decision to share in the name of disdain. It takes no more energy to think loving thoughts than it does to think harmful ones. The assumption that as long as the person doesn't hear our criticism we're not harming him or her is spiritually inaccurate. This presumption is spiritually unsound because thought transmits just like radio waves. Reception can be picked up by anyone attuned to your frequency, including the message you have just transmitted. Thought travels; thought never dies; it is part of the imprint of our lives--indestructible, universal. I have conversed with many of the dearly departed who have shared the message of astonishment in discovering that their lives were recorded and reviewed once humans die and reach the other side. Those who've committed suicide have quickly related the message, "The joke's on me; I have escaped nothing." Many have relayed their astonishment at how life continues, the opportunity to grow never ends, and examination of one's life is inevitable.

The evidence showing that we humans start our life review prior to death is quite astonishing. Psychological research now proves that each person in the advanced stages of dying goes through this process regardless of their resistance to or awareness of it. The book, *On Death and Dying*, by psychiatrist Elizabeth Kubler-Ross, M.D. is an amazing resource. Dr. Raymond Moody discusses many case histories in his classic, *Life After Life*. I watched my dying mother straighten pictures on the wall at least ten times an hour. I watched my former mother-in-law focus on one of her favorite drawings and tell me stories by the hour of all the things that were happening in the picture. Both of these women were reviewing. My mother absolutely did not want to die and was in denial about putting her life in order. My former mother-in-law took a more gentle approach to her death and lovingly reviewed her existence with dignity and grace. Each of us will determine how we die and each of us, upon arriving at the other side, will experience in totality the awareness of every act of *love* and every act *absent* of love that we have ever shared with this world.

Why not start now being virtuous, loving, and kind and giving your neighbors the benefit of the doubt? The truth is we will have a far more enjoyable time during our life review on both sides of the veil if we just make this attempt. The discipline is simple. In the presence of negativity, **balk** at the idea of joining in. I assure you there is no Saint Peter waiting at the pearly gates, yet there is your Soul and your consciousness waiting to start the review the minute you arrive. Because free will reigns, you can stall the procedure until your mood improves, but before spiritual advancement can take place you will have to go through the process.

In most cases when I have sought interaction with a departed love one on behalf of a client, the departed is in full agreement to participate in the communication. Most have turned towards the light of salvation and understanding, doing whatever it takes to accept personal accountability at all times, so that the process of advancement can continue. Many spirits find the courage to follow their bliss and engage in activity suited to them. It's the same thing they longed to do in human life but were too afraid. Parental, religious, and social pressure often took precedence. Regret is hardly mentioned; optimism and the encouragement to be self-realized are usually interjected in their messages to their loved ones here on earth.

When skepticism and the need for proof enter the mind of a client, the departed rarely validates his or her own authenticity. I believe it's because the client has an attachment to legitimacy instead of wanting to comprehend the loved one's present situation and message. Everyone's mindset is transmitted throughout the universe and anyone who is paying attention receives the message. When I act as a go between and receive the attention of the deceased, the deceased readily comprehends the sincerity level of his or her relatives or loved ones here on earth. Sincerity often prompts a "zinger." The Spirit of the deceased shares a tidbit or two of information so confirming and validating that never again will the earthbound doubt the deceased's ongoing existence. Once in awhile I encounter negativity and lack of optimism from spirits. Their free will is obviously still focused on regret, fear, and distrust. They are uncomfortable with their surroundings often because they still subscribe to earthly beliefs concerning punishment awaiting those who have participated in evil, uncaring deeds in life. Their lack of progress is their self-inflicted punishment. Spirits are quick to remind us that the other side is full of choice just like we have here on earth.

Whenever you are in a situation where negativity is spewing out of the mouths of those around you, create a loving defense by erecting an imaginary shield between you and the offending parties. This reminder is a focal point which keeps you in touch with the real responsibilities of life. Give everyone the benefit of the doubt. Ask yourself in all situations: " What would love do here and now?" and realize that your seeming *lack of action* will yield positive results when you ultimately choose to be accountable for every deed, action and word you have shared with life.

I like to imagine myself in a pink bubble as a reminder of the heart being my greatest ally with regard to loving acts. I gently swim in this pink bubble; it safeguards me from negative energy in my surroundings, which by now feels cold and sterile from my new vantage point. If I'm being tempted more than usual to engage in non-positive conversation, I keep saying to myself over and over: "I uphold the truth" or "Come from love." Any phrase rich in affirmation of what I desire to do helps keep me on track and out of the grips of temptation. By practicing this discipline you'll eventually free your time and energy to engage in creative, positive, productive interactions which enhance the quality of all life.

Chapter Thirteen

Being vs. Doing

"No one can make you feel inferior without your consent."

-Eleanor Roosevelt

Each one of us becomes proficient at life when we balance our focus between earth and Spirit. In order to focus upon Spirit, we have to move out of a regime called *doing* long enough to let our attention drift both outward and inward beyond the confines of the five-sense world into a place called *being*. This mystical place called Spirit is only recognized when we are still enough in the hearts and minds to comprehend its glory. What happens in the state of being is always mysterious because the language there is rarely spoken. It is usually felt in a very precise, often uplifting, manner. Being is the place where we can experience renewal, inspiration, insight, and unconditional positive regard.

The Universal Mind regards each of us as perfect and whole; guilt, shame, and low self-esteem are never experienced in this state of grace. It is equivalent to amnesia with regard to all the negative thoughts and emotions about self. In being we can open the door to reflection, yet it is from a benign perspective. The idea of crucifying ourselves over errant ways is foreign to the real art of being. Stillness and quiet are the main points of reference. This ushers in awareness of what is going on in our inner world. The second great attribute after awareness is acceptance of that about which an individual becomes aware.

Awareness can only be attained when the mind drops--to the best of its ability--the need to define, use, or declare the importance of what the senses register. This seemingly impossible task can be attained and has often been associated with spiritual disciplines of the East. Awareness leads to expansion. Take, for example, the observation of a chair. If we limit the experience of the chair in front of us to a definition of furniture only, then we have limited awareness. If instead we view this piece as fire-starting material, a work of art, texture, shape, size, potential comfort, color, or fifty other ways of exercising our awareness, then we are in a state of being with the chair. Rigid thinking is a difficult persuasion to drop, especially if an individual has been steeped in this programming from early childhood. Yet in order to attain awareness, we must strive for expansive, unlimited thinking. Awareness is like waking up our minds, which choose thoughts that go down the same grooves hour after hour. Unless they strive for awareness, humans will never know the exhilarating joy of the quiet mind, which can drink in all that the senses have to offer.

Once awareness of the natural world is measured with some degree of accuracy, awareness of the supernatural begins to call the spiritual seeker. There is a human inclination in each of us to know what the other side is like. We've seen depictions in movies and heard the compelling tales of those who have experienced "near-death awakenings." Each of us longs in our Spirit to remember "home," the place of personal creation. In the solitude and surrender one opens to the mysteries of awareness because of the comfort they bring. There is great contentment in knowing that a space of unconditional love exists. Feeling and knowing this space is like quenching an intensive thirst. The most interesting aspect of this exercise is the ease of practice. All one really needs to do is focus; that's all there is to it. In many ancient traditions the subject of focus has been on the breath. It really doesn't matter what you use as long as you remain attentive to the exercise. Being in the state of awareness implies nothing more than gathering in all the runaway thoughts and substituting one for them. This gives the mind a chance to surrender. Once reached, the supernatural world is easy, light, and full of ongoing rewards.

The main reward of feeling accepted is this: we begin to regain our courage and self-esteem. The goal of being in cosmic acceptance is to let it filter into all phases of our human experience so that we not only accept ourselves--including the actions, thoughts and feelings of our lives--but also all life around us. Sometimes this task seems insurmountable because we're always asking the question: "How can I accept the intolerable, inhumane, insane activities of others?" The easiest way to achieve this is to practice letting go of any attachment to "what should be." Buddha said that at this point we are the slaves of the clinging mind which is the source of all unhappiness. Each new time the choice to exhibit a state of attainment is undertaken, the task gets easier and easier for there is no finer guideline or state of existence than that of awakening, especially to the awareness of being in the presence of Unconditional Love.

Try this experiment the next time you are exasperated and out of sorts, for they are sure signs that you have strayed from the practice of being focused, present in the moment, and aware of Spirit. First, give yourself permission to feel all of your discomfort. When any need to act on it arises, simply say to yourself: "This can wait." Next, ask yourself this question: "Whose permission do I need to feel good again?" With accurate, truthful evaluation of the situation, your only legitimate answer will be: "My own." After acknowledging your feelings and remembering who's in charge, it is easier to search for any superficiality surrounding how seriously you've taken the event that caused the discomfort in the first place. At this point you're ready to return to a state of being which contains the magnificence of Unconditional Love, reduced tension, and expanded awareness. Now focus on just this one phrase: "I am peaceful." If you stick to this mindfully, temptation to return to a state of being upset will slowly vanish. A return to loving acceptance is often the surprising result of this experiment.

Doing is the antithesis of being and is a major component in the process of every human life. Every individual has been given a special and unique purpose to fulfill during each lifetime. The wonderful truth is that our Spirit wants to lead us down this path all the time and our higher consciousness wants to give us direction and courage to do so. The United States, as well as other progressive nations, has been on a major "doing" regime for the last one hundred and twenty years or so. More industrial, scientific, and technological advancements have been made in this short span of history than in the whole previous history of civilization. The acceleration in the race for achievement leaves most of us in a state of imbalance. In the name of efficiency, comfort, and speed, the pipeline to Spirit has shriveled or been severed completely. From the gnawing need to keep doing, a national tragedy has arisen. A hunger and thirst for something invisible is striking the hearts of citizens by the millions. This void can only be defined as *spiritual deficiency*, better known as alienation from the Source. It is a major cause of anxiety and tension, which ultimately leads to depression and regret. **Without practicing being, fulfilling the contract of doing becomes exasperating**. When an individual slows down, focuses, and has the courage to meditate, energy is renewed and the insight to achieve goals with greater competency arises.

James is a doer. He constantly looks for the right job that contains the quickest advancement and the least amount of conflict and disagreement. He wants to sail through each day making sure he makes sales, fulfills quotas, and impresses his superiors. He is on his third job within a year and has sought my advice before each one in order to find out what his compatibility in the workplace might be like. I constantly remind him that he can learn in any situation because any one of the sales positions he seeks offers the potential for him to make money, advance in rank, and satisfy his quest for security. James is learning that it isn't the job that holds him back, but his attitude and beliefs. When each of us is still and quiet concerning the potential decision to make, we begin to internally discern which action contains the best possibilities to meet our goal. With James, attempts to consult his higher guidance concerning the best path to take cause confusion and uncertainty with regard to the insights he receives.

The reason for lack of clarity has to do with subconscious programming that overrides the information he receives. This man's major negative beliefs about self are: "I can only get ahead if I work hard," and "If you get close to someone, you'll get hurt." Both of these beliefs were created by his subconscious because he was taught as a child that both are true for every human being. He struggles at the job believing it's all wrong and the people are disagreeable, thus justifying his decision to leave. Even if I suggested that he stay where he is, it would not override his subconscious desire to create struggle in his life. Only by returning to the fertile playground of being can this man regain the perspective he needs. If he chooses to become aware that other ways of conduct foster positive results, he might find it easier to stay on the job. Positive conduct can be created through affirmations and by imaging himself working easily and fearlessly.

Affirmations are a powerful form of self-talk and remind the subconscious what we presently want out of life. Self-talk makes definitive statements of the condition we want to exist now and in every subsequent moment. Imagery takes into account the activation of all the inner senses. This process includes a dress rehearsal where we see, hear, and feel who and what we want to become. When images are experienced passionately with faith and conviction, they can usher in a new belief system more quickly. Adding gusto to an affirmation, such as a definitive statement of who we now believe we are, immensely speeds up the process of reprogramming the subconscious. James's concept of himself working more easily can be practiced over and over in his mind until it manifests the affirmation in his physical world. "I accept the accolades and compliments of others and I'm undaunted by criticism and negative display of emotions" transforms fear into fearlessness. I constantly remind my client that his fear of getting hurt is imagined. He felt this imagined fear in his heart and chose to make it real;

therefore, physical as well as emotional pain emerged whenever the words or deeds of another appeared negative. In order to offset his fear of being hurt I encouraged him to raise his self-esteem. The easiest way of doing this is through positive self-talk and imagining situations where the criticism or abandonment of others is not destructive. The key is to remember times when the positive, life-giving opinion of ourselves is more important than any outside one. Risk becomes easier as we rely on inner strength and opinion as opposed to those outside of us. My client embraced the understanding that he often got the jump on those he was fearful of. At the first sign of someone's being discourteous, critical or agitating, James would immediately look for excuses to avoid his or her company. Avoidance is a surefire sign that fear is prevalent. James was tired of running so he decided to work with these suggestions.

At this point you're probably saying to yourself, "I would leave too if someone was heckling me." Leaving anything from the perspective of fear only draws a similar scene back into our lives. In these cases the Universal Intelligence asks us to do one thing: **be true to ourselves**. Part of this truth always lies in our ability to be fearless. Leaving from the standpoint of neutrality is far better than leaving out of fear, even though we long to stand behind the pretense: "I don't have to stand for this kind of behavior." There is a fine line between self-assertion and self-defeat. Self-assertion says, "I can stay because I can handle the situation or I can leave because being here no longer serves me." The right to come and go is part of our free will package, yet leaving because we lack the wherewithal to withstand the aggravation of another only prompts us to test ourselves somewhere else. Part of being true to oneself is standing up under fire, claiming strength, and standing in it wholeheartedly. Remember, if we don't learn the lesson, we'll repeat it until we do.

James had a very disagreeable first marriage, claiming that his wife was mentally incompetent and unfit as a mother. He was able to win custody of their child and start a new life.

Unfortunately, he brought forward his distrust for women, fearing that they could hurt and malign him as his wife once did. The truth is that each person must forgo the risk of rejection in order to reap the rewards of love. My client longed desperately for a healthy, long-term, loving relationship with a female, yet his belief that it would take a lot of hard work and subject him to possible rejection stood in his way. He understood that this belief lies just below the surface in his subconscious, so he started the process of **doing** in his imagination. He found a woman who is not mentally or emotionally available, a similar scenario to his marriage, yet he is willing to remain friends with her, which prompts them to practice trust, patience and acceptance. Instead of running away, he persists at practicing **being** with her, yet **doing** something quite different from before. James now listens to her without telling her what to do, affirms her, and moves back into self-awareness when he notices that his attitude towards her is becoming conditional. Best of all, he practices self-acceptance by imagining that he is always doing the best he can in any given situation or moment.

Chapter Fourteen

Monitor What Persists

"Opportunities are often things you haven't noticed the first time around."

-Catherine Deneuve

The world around us is a classroom. Every moment of our lives we have the opportunity to learn lessons that foster peace or chaos. The key instrument with the experiment of life is our Higher Self. This energy is the intelligence of our Soul and has no substitute. It demands nothing yet will help us set up in the physical, exterior world any life opportunities that will envelope us in peace and harmony. So you ask, "Why is this state so desirable?" The answer is simple. The ability to love and the opportunity to live one's truth comes about easier when the body, mind, and emotions are content and satisfied. Excessive longing and desire prompt the Creative Forces to teach us a lesson. Christian Scripture says, "Thou shalt have no other gods before Me." False gods carry with them the theme of longing which often persists and persists and persists. I believe the Force that created us makes one and only one request: "Follow your happiness." Purpose and happiness are always coexistent. In order for bliss to prevail, one must take stock in one's natural tendencies so that purpose will surface and be willingly followed. Anyone indifferent to his or her specific purpose will never achieve bliss.

False gods are like trains of thought driven by demands contrary to one's main task. These thoughts usually center on ambitions, needs, status, and power which only serve to boost the ego. The ego is an internal device created to perpetuate the concept of separation. Success often fosters the concept of being better than or the idea of being more powerful than. It is easy to persist in perpetuating these lies, and our addiction to them continues the creation of false self-esteem, a condition common to humans. **God would have us be true to our purpose, not our power.** Paradoxically those who are most alive and blissfully follow their purposes exemplify the greatest display of natural power. These folks are alive, pulsating with enthusiasm and a zest for life. At the same time they are at peace because the war within has ended. These individuals no longer think of themselves as superior to others, thus freeing up the time formerly used to convince others of their superiority. As healthy humans, they can now engage in more worthwhile activity congruent with their purpose.

Whatever returns again and again as a lesson in the classroom of life is no accident. Each persisting subject constitutes a solid reminder of what we have made a god. Tom wants to be appreciated by his girlfriend. Is this an outlandish request from any man who chooses to be in a romantic relationship with another? Of course the answer is "no;" everyone desires to be honored by his or her partner for the talents of consideration, ability to focus, and commitment. Often Tom crosses into the world of aggravation because his girlfriend is not appreciative of him in desired ways. He keeps score of when she does and does not comply with his internal demands of her. For years he has dealt with a persistent reoccurring theme of betrayal in his life. Women are not there for him when he needs them the most, or so it seems according to his perception.

Specifically Tom was looking for a woman who would sense his frustrations with work and coworkers. He wanted someone who would hold him tenderly and, without saying a word, make the world feel safer and less caustic. He wanted his female partner to be patient and kind as he vented his frustrations. The action that he desired, as opposed to someone trying to tell him what to do, was that of rubbing his taut shoulders, stroking his head and hair, or taking him on a walk to further work out his kinks. He dreamed of her leaving him little notes of encouragement, whispering sweet nothings late at night, or preparing his favorite dessert. He also welcomed surprise phone calls, romantic evening curled on the couch watching a movie, or her showing some small interest in his hobbies or latest play toy. Not all men appear to want these simple gestures bestowed upon them, but I assure you away from the macho crowd, they represent a cross section of the actual needs most authentic men have.

To have a better chance at receiving what you want, I offer a two-fold discipline. First, isolate what is missing in your relationship with another, and then practice exemplifying with him or her that very same quality for thirty days. The classroom then becomes not only a learning center for you but a teaching forum as well. By focusing on voluntarily giving the quality you're looking for from another, you're less likely to be a grouch because you are doing something in place of feeling cheated. Because the freedom to think with less attachment has arisen, more opportunity to see the previously undetected, positive behavior and affirmation of your beloved begins to surface in your thoughts.

Tom tried this and was amazed at his resistance. It was difficult to switch gears and listen to the internal voice of giving instead of the one that insidiously demanded. He was so trained to look at the missing pieces that there was no praise for her even when his preferences were satisfied. He had made a god of his determination and ability to point out all of his girlfriend's flaws. This thinking not only included his present love connection but also all prior romantic involvements. Tom persisted in cultivating the art of pointing out flaws, dissecting them point by point, and always making sure each was completely exposed and accounted for when confronting his girlfriends.

From a spiritual perspective this behavior is primarily a waste of time. It camouflages higher wishes. What Tom longs to do is share parts of himself, which his family never encouraged. He is ultimately being challenged by his Higher Self and the Universal Mind to find the courage to express his true feelings.

The second part of the discipline is quite simple. Share your joy, adulation, excitement, fear, disappointment, and discouragement instead of your persistent camouflage. Pouting or pointing fingers, instead of taking care of the business of speaking your truth, creates more and more lessons. When Tom is giving attention to the art of being truthful with his feelings, he is automatically encouraging his girlfriend to do likewise. Even if after thirty days he achieves no influence at all over the situation by being a model example, he will still have the satisfaction of feeling good about himself, which will make future relationships much more rewarding. If Tom goes into them with more honesty in his heart, then he, according to the laws of Spirit, will receive more heartfelt interaction in return.

We are dealing with a unique and important universal law here--the law of giving and receiving. What we give out, be it negative or positive, is going to come back to us. The catch is this: when, where and how the energy we put out comes back will always be a mystery. The person we gift may or may not return in like manor the love we give out, yet service becomes its own reward. As Tom gives lovingly from his heart, he stays positive, reduces stress, has more time for personal interests, and will--at some unappointed time and place—be gifted with all the positive energy he is showing to his girlfriend. If he shares his feelings, the world will ultimately do so in return.

The God of love demands **not** that we be constant examples of love, yet if we aren't, a lesson in the classroom of life created by us becomes our destiny.

Chapter Fifteen

Practice Giving from the Heart

"We who lived in concentration camps can remember the men who walked through the huts comforting others, giving away their last piece of bread. They may have been few in number, but they offer sufficient proof that everything can be taken from a man but one thing: the last of human freedoms—to choose one's attitude in any given set of circumstances—to choose one's own way."

-Victor Frankl

The easiest test to determine if we give from the heart is to observe how we deal with beggars, commonly known in our culture as panhandlers. The common excuse we hear when someone refuses to give is this: "If I knew that the beggar was going to get food or something useful, I would give." I'm happy when I see people like this keep their hands out of their pockets because the giving would not have been from the heart. Heartfelt giving looks for nothing after the experience. This giver honors the receiver's ability to make unlimited use of the gift. Most of us know the beggar's chances of spending this money at the corner liquor store or with the local drug dealer might be very high. Our job, as part of the giving process, is to accept, to the best of our abilities, whatever choice the receiver makes with his newfound bounty.

One night my dinner companion and I were taking a leisurely stroll after our meal. As we walked, we passed a young man in a wheelchair, and for no apparent reason we stopped in front of him for one brief moment. Our stopping offered him just enough window of opportunity to speak up and ask, "Could you help me get into a shelter down the street?" In my naiveté I assumed that he wanted us to push him down to the Salvation Army, and I was immediately looking forward to the exercise. My friend obviously knew this young man had another intention in mind, and he immediately began to search his pocket. It finally dawned on me the real nature of this man's request, so I began to fumble around for dollar bills also. As a combined effort, we handed over a five-dollar bill. Without a smile or thank you, the man made a further request that we stuff the bill into his sock which my companion immediately did. He then turned and started to walk away. Before I could leave, the panhandler asked me if I had enjoyed my dinner and once again, naively, I said, "Yes." At this point my friend grabbed my arm and without saying a word steered me down the street. As we got out of hearing range of the wheelchair-bound, young man, my friend told me that the man wanted more money and this was his way of informing us. My friend was also quick to note, "He did not give a verbal or physical gesture of thanks."

Any time we expect something after giving has taken place, we break ties with the unconditionality of our act. One of the main reasons for mental disturbance is the accumulated disappointment and grief felt by humans because they have not been rewarded for their charity. Whenever an agenda exists in our minds concerning what needs to take place after the act of giving, it can be damaging to our health, specifically in three ways. First, it draws our attention away from the present moment; it is easy to obsess on what should have been. Secondly, it promotes self-esteem based on outside gratification instead of inner approval, and thirdly, it causes us to waste time by entering into negativity and spreading it each time we complain about the incident.

A few months later I was casually walking with my son on the same street. Another panhandler was sitting on the curb looking dismayed and wanting to know if we would give him some money. He shared the news that he was down on his luck, was new in town, was unemployed, and sure was hungry. Without the slightest bit of hesitation, my son whipped out a ten-dollar bill and gave it to him. My son went on to explain to me how grateful he was that he had a good job and was in a position to share. He relayed that he felt good in his heart that he had given and seemed little concerned about how the man would spend the money. He turned to me and said, "Dad, I'm so blessed because I have a job I love which doesn't seem like work at all. I have friends and family, and I'm respected in my profession. What more could I ask for?" In that instant I felt rather funny because earlier, as the man was talking, my mind chatter was going something like this: "Does this guy really mean it?" Then, after my son's act of kindness, I was questioning, "Can my son really afford this?"

After a few moments of reflection, it occurred to me to ask myself who was wearing the spiritual pants in our family on this occasion. I've come to learn that a request for anything is a test to measure our unconditionality in the moment. Each experience is a unique experiment in selflessness. All of us have a mental idea of how unconditionally giving we can be. The Universe wants to know how close we can really be to this ideal, so it gives us chances over and over again. I had my opportunity a few days later.

I was sitting at a red light in the middle of a busy intersection. A man with a sign, similar to ones I had seen a hundred times before, was in front of me in the median. I had always detested these signs because they made no sense to me at all. "Homeless," "Will Work for Pay," etc., etc. seemed so dishonest. I always thought that honesty might be the best policy, so the simple words, "I Need Money," or "Can You Help Me?", might be more convincing. It suddenly dawned on me that their poor marketing was my problem and not theirs. If donations were poor, I doubt they would be on the corner using this sign day after day in appealing to the sympathy of others. So in reality their marketing strategy was not so bad after all. On this particular occasion instead of trying to figure out how this man might spend his money, I found myself--almost without thinking--reaching into my pocket and handing him a five-dollar bill. Waves of peace and personal satisfaction gently washed over me, and I knew in that instant that I was practicing the fine art of giving from the heart.

Giving without strings is an exciting adventure which is ultimately more fruitful than we can usually imagine. Selfless giving opens us to feelings of godliness that have no substitute. The reward for this kind of giving is unique unto itself because we feel good through and through. There is no hesitation about how the gift will be received or what use will be made of it later. The next time the impulse to give emerges from left field, take heart and give from this special, sacred place within you. Also be aware of every time the mind wants to sabotage the simple gesture because scarcity issues dominate your belief in the moment. Measure the degree of mind chatter that would keep saying, "No, no, no-- the gift might be used improperly, or there may be lack of respect or appreciation for me, the giver." Every day we reenact this sad scenario with family, a significant other, children, friends, and associates.

The heart feels expansion each time one of us bypasses the fear of giving. Giving signals trust in our capacity to surround ourselves with the fruits of our labor, which can then be divided among our neighbors. Giving is what Creator has done for us. Life's ultimate gift has been our Humanity given freely to us by Divine Intelligence. We have also been given a wonderful sanctuary called planet Earth. Each time we give unconditionally we reenact the creation story again and again, for we are created to live freely and unencumbered in a world that profits each time we give from the heart.

The next time you're put into a position to give or not give, consider the following exercise. Ask your mind to please suspend its activity long enough for you to gain insight. Imagine that you turn off a switch in the back of your head and the mind goes blank. Next check your body sensations. Are you tense, annoyed, or anxious? If so, chances are you're motivated by guilt and frustration--guilt because you have the means to give and frustration because you don't believe it's fair for "them" to have put you in this position in the first place. Gently move through your emotional reactions by honoring them and at the same time recognizing their superficiality. This part of the process lets you slowly access your heart of hearts. Third, breathe a few deep breaths imagining that your tension will completely exit by the end of the fourth or fifth exhalation. Go beyond your mind and contrived emotions to experience a signal from your Higher Self. Look for thoughts being spoken in your head, strong, undaunted feelings that can be translated into a message, or notice that an inner vision might be taking place in your *mind's eye*. Fourth, register whatever washes over you from a more truthful and sincere place within your consciousness. Decide to trust this insight and find the courage to act upon it in this situation. You may be very surprised at your soulful response to what you previously considered a nagging problem.

Chapter Sixteen

Make It Light

*"Life is a game; play it.
Life is love; share it.
Life is a challenge; meet it.
Life is a dream; realize it."*

-*Sathya Sai Baba*

Levity, according to Webster, has to do with an attitude characterized by lack of seriousness. It also concerns the reality of having "little weight." When we address life from this standpoint, we began to reduce our troubles considerably. Being lighthearted about any situation in no way implies discounting its reality.

What happens in place of worry, anger or pain when an event is put into a more lighthearted perspective? First of all, we recognize that the Universe and its Infinite Wisdom are far more than we can ascertain. Secondly, we realize that just because we are privileged to information doesn't mean we're to do a darn thing about it. We're given access to events and activities around us to practice the art of non-attachment and to see how well we hold up spiritually. Deciding to get involved just because someone is hurting can be a violation of that person's space, possibly preventing him or her from engaging in important lessons. Humor, like non-attachment, is a valuable tool, preventing us from taking life so seriously that we doubt God's miraculous, protective power. I believe that anyone can be safe if he or she is willing to extend love, especially to one's self. Those who take themselves super seriously have forgotten both their purpose and their place in the Universe.

Let's take Brian, for example. He is suspicious of everyone in his work place, constantly fearing that his job is in jeopardy. Any hint of control, admonishment, or critical review exercised by another person makes Brian crazy. He is afraid of being used and abused by his superiors. It is also true that this man fears giving because he might not receive an adequate return on his investment, and he is so anti-control that he can't even practice it on himself. He lets his suspicious thoughts and negative emotions run away with him, most often using them as a basis for unhealthy decision-making. This man claims that he is constantly ready to bolt from his present job and into a place that's safer. My reassurance was to remind him that he is the author of his own safety. Leaving his present job would be no guarantee that he would be treated differently elsewhere. If Brian could listen openly to the suggestions of his superiors and remember their usefulness, he might have less fear of control.

Levity is a missing ingredient for Brian because he was taught to keep his mouth shut, never question authority, always play by the rules, and follow instructions without question. This set the stage for a great dichotomy within. As Brian got older and began to mature, he realized his own ability to make decisions and think for himself. He also felt the prompting of his own Spirit leading him in the direction of his own drumbeat. On the other hand, he was being bombarded with demands to follow authority.

Every day of his life Brian faces thousands of decisions to either follow his subconscious programming (internalized demands) or follow his heart. Anger and frustration arise because he is never sure if his decisions will turn out well or even if he owns the right to make them. His internal programming says: "Rely on the outside for 'they know better.'" His Higher Self says, "Trust your innate wisdom, laugh at life's paradoxes, and dare to live your truth." Each time a person laughs at the power previously given to the past, it frees up the present scene. Instead of being heavy with burden or guilt, freedom is acquired prompting decisions pertinent to the moment and nothing else. When we take ourselves too seriously, we try to either control the world around us or ourselves to such a heavy degree that life becomes almost impossible. Brian over-inflates his importance and is driven by a mile-high ego. Why else would he spend so much time worrying about how he should be treated instead of how he can most lovingly treat life around him? The self-absorbed person uses the opinions of the outside world as a camouflage to cover his or her potential and squelch the right to freedom.

Today witness some major plunge undertaken by you into over-seriousness. Imagine how you would feel if you had just observed a video of the event. Observe the obvious self-importance but without condemnation. Chances are you might laugh wholeheartedly at your self-absorption concerning an activity that no longer has much importance.

Chapter Seventeen

Refresh Your Body

*"I believe in the flesh and the appetites;
Seeing, hearing, feeling, are miracles and
Each part and tag of me is a miracle."*

-Walt Whitman

One of the main complaints I hear as a counselor is this: "I just don't have enough time to get everything done; I'm so stressed out." Why has this phenomenon proliferated in a society of such wealth and privilege? Millions are driven by some insane need to prove themselves. Internal estimation of one's usefulness, talent, and capability is often so lacking that constant striving to receive acknowledgement and praise from the outside world is necessary. The gain of material wealth--not because it's a fun game and available, but because it's a statement of self worth--has become a national tragedy. This need keeps people on the move and often highly restricts their leisure time.

The business world often takes advantage of human insecurity, seeing human output as an expendable commodity and often viewing humans as disposable as napkins. A lack of regard for the complete person helps fragment the individual, prompting feelings of security only in areas of business expertise. This fragmentation creates an annoying suspicion that parts of the personality, body, intellect or emotional life that are not used or acknowledged on the job are inadequate. To handle the constant strain put upon us by unhealthy business objectives, experiences of relaxation and rejuvenation are a must.

I was recently engaged in a conversation with a client about the nature of reality. Julie's concept of reality is that she has total control over--far in advance of their occurrence--all the activities of her life. I reminded her that there are many forms of reality, including illusionary ones. Reality is the inclusion of thought as well as the occurrence of what is. Everything is being thought up all the time. Minds are thinking up new ideas and focusing, always focusing, thus creating new realities. In the real world there are billions of similar chain reactions going on all the time. All this thought activity creates the universal world, the "what is" experience.

Internal drama and conflict started to take place when Julie's perception of her personal capability to take control in the physical world became distorted. The spiritual formula for life teaches that Julie has control over everything from her skin inward--in other words, her inner world of personal creation. The Universal Mind, with its ability to shine favorably on millions of personal dreams all at one time, is in control of everything from Julie's skin line outward. In other words, it contains the raw material for all that we desire. This Mind also knows the perfect timing, mindset, and circumstances to bring about our desires.

Frustration comes when this Universal Truth is neglected or ignored. The mental and emotional strain, which ultimately transfers to the body, can be avoided when a clear delineation of power is understood. Julie is responsible for herself and her dreams; the Universe is responsible for carrying out her dreams as well as all other dreams held fast in the consciousness of mankind. Julie admits to forgetting to practice what she knows about physical reality. She is aware of her stress when she tries to control what is outside of herself.

The body can be refreshed every time a decision to let go of what cannot be controlled arises. An automatic reduction in tension, stress, and anxiety occurs when we do. Julie breathes easier every time she remembers that she is in charge of her life and hers alone. A good way to handle the buildup of stress is either to sit quietly for a few moments or create purposeful distraction such as a walk or comic relief. When this woman sits quietly she begins to remember what she is made of, and glimmers of Divine Love and Power flow through her awareness. These make up for the mind's inadequacies, which limit awareness of love and power within.

The mind demands: "Follow a more mature route to security by going for a job that offers more salary, no matter what the sacrifices in time and energy." By not pursuing her passions, which are in the field of artistic expression, she misses out on enjoyment. This compounds the self-esteem issue. This occurs when she blindly follows the mind, denying her what is deeply appealing and healthy. When Julie forgets her power, she automatically feels stuck and inadequate. This translates into letting others advise her instead of being advised by the still, small voice within. Julie's fear of sitting alone in quiet and peace is that the ghosts of her past will haunt her. When thoughts of failure, prompted by being passed over more than once for a promotion, arise, they can pose a devastating threat to an already fragile self-concept.

Every time an unflattering, inaccurate opinion crosses the mind in these periods of rest and solitude, a new challenge arises. Instead of feeling despair, disturbance, or projection, it is far better to remember times when love is flowing and power is felt. Confidence is restored as Julie dwells on the positive accomplishments and feelings of Divine Energy flowing within. **The impetus to do this is remembered by focusing on a preordained word, which triggers the initial decision to think lovingly about oneself.** Her word is canvas, which elicits a vivid scene in her imagination. Her mind's eye sees a canvas, larger-than-life, with her smiling victoriously as painting after painting sells. The security of owning a dream, focusing on accomplishment, and knowing its victory is a simple way of overcoming the darkness found in silence.

Physical movement is an easy way to change the body's tempo. For example, going for a walk is a signal that resolution is ahead. When I walk it is a great tension calmer because the activity reminds me of how life actually operates. All life is going forward with creative momentum. As I walk every afternoon or just before bedtime, it is as if I leave behind old, spent energy, like a snake shedding its skin. The feelings of new possibilities charge me and renew my mind. I have time to let a voice inside lovingly relate to my most perfect paths. I don't always hear the voice of truth, yet I find it easier to discern it when I am walking. On my short sojourns I try to focus on all the nature around me, ever present to her quiet, accepting ways. I feast on the natural beauty that Great Creator has provided for me every time I get out of my mind and into the flow of life. When I no longer need to focus on my world, I automatically glimpse the other real one where God's love abounds.

One of the most amazing attributes of life exists when we are sane enough to laugh at our folly. Making healthy light of a mistake is far more useful than condemnation. A negative reaction to anything compounds the problem. If Julie decides to condemn herself for screwing up at the office, her subconscious mind will add this negative reaction to a memory bank. What happens next is that she compounds her present mistake by bringing up all of her past putdowns from the deep recesses of her mind. Unbeknownst to Julie, she still lives with indecision regarding past judgments. A healthy evaluation would tell her to rise above judgment, yet her negativity is prompting her to self-evaluate in a lowly manner. Giving regard to negative self-talk or negative evaluation from another slows the process of regaining self-esteem and acts as a detriment in the creation of self-love.

It is very easy to make a decision to think lightheartedly about a perceived mistake. All it takes is a quick reevaluation of dedication. If this dedication is towards forgiveness and a cosmic perspective concerning behavior, then a quick mental reevaluation can be accomplished in a split second. I can laugh about my folly or I can compound my self-dislike.

The stacking effect of one negative evaluation upon another is what causes the Spirit to break. The truth is that Spirit never breaks, but we, as humans, break from its goodness and truth. Our Higher Consciousness will remind us of this. We are love, and if this is so, our main obligation remains firm. We must stop condemning our actions immediately.

The next time Julie is faced with the decision to self-condemn or lighten up, she can more easily choose the latter by imagining herself as a clown in the most absurd clown outfit she has ever seen. This can easily trigger her prior decision to focus on her folly with laughter and good humor. By following this exercise I'm not suggesting that Julie camouflage her feelings by pretending that everything is "all right." She may be thoroughly embarrassed by her lack of expertise, but personal choice is the point in question. In any given moment, everyone has a choice to negatively exaggerate a situation or put it into spiritual context. Through instant forgiveness, total acceptance, and a return to the moment, each of us instantly propels oneself into higher states of consciousness, simultaneously reducing the residual effects of what we negatively term as a blunder, mistake or act of stupidity. Julie's usual reaction was: "I should have known better." Repeating this remark keeps her stuck. Constant repetition of negative self-talk emphasizes what we are **not** instead of what we are.

After a blunder the most important thing for Julie to do is imagine herself in a scene experiencing a perfect performance. Repeating this image in a non-judgmental, loving way constitutes the best insurance any of us have regarding doing something well. The only way Julie will ever achieve permanent success is to envision it ahead of time and have her thoughts geared toward worthiness. By making light of a situation, out of choice, there is less distance to cover between low self-esteem and internal worth. This relief affects the body in very positive ways. Stress levels go down, blood pressure goes down, and feelings of being centered and assured are ultimate results of the exercise.

Chapter Eighteen

Give More Than You Are Required

"True wealth is measured not by what we leave behind but by what we can afford to give away before we go."

-Forrest Church

I've worked with many students who pride themselves on being gracious givers, yet with close observation, few elements of unconditional giving can actually be detected. The discipline of giving more than we have previously planned shows conclusively how truly willing we are to give unconditionally. During a particularly difficult financial period of my life, I was upset about how child support money was being spent. I was displeased with my former wife's spending habits, especially with regard to our son's college education. I complained and created internal upset whenever I thought about the subject, and I was mad at the loss of control. After a couple of months of harboring resentment, I ventured inward to ask guidance for advice.

Guidance is a natural aid, a gift from Creator available to every human being. The most important thing to know about guidance is this: use is more important than structure. One of the most frequently asked questions concerning guidance is this: "What if I contact unhealthy, unreliable guidance that would lead me astray?" I believe firmly that anyone who is dedicated to living a healthy, spiritually clean life will attract guidance capable of enhancing well being. Good people attract good guidance. Every human spirit inherently seeks the most godly path and perfect action for himself or herself. When human intention is at least in part authored by a willingness to give unconditionally, then guidance automatically seeks to share the most effective ways to do this.

I believe the Spirit realm accommodates each of us when it comes to form. Victoria believes Mother Mary guides her. Donald trusts his guardian angel, while Alexander envisions the Buddha is around him all the time. Robert channels a guide called Oliver, while Mary allows a star being called Omnia to use her internal computer and intelligence to allow its message to be spoken by her. For over ten years the Spirit of Guiseppe poured forth his wisdom through me every day. In my early days I would agonize over the authenticity of this Spirit being because I did not want to share some fantasy of my imagination with the general public. I've since come to recognize the mystery surrounding these intelligences needs to remain sacred. Today it is the accuracy and usefulness of their message that is most important to me.

Robert A. Johnson's book, *Inner Work: Using Dreams and Active Imagination for Personal Growth*, is a fascinating exposé that helps explain the inner guidance from the psychological perspective. We thrive by utilizing the information we receive. Accurately comprehending and courageously following through on this information are the most useful objectives of guidance. Laboring over the authenticity of guides and questioning their reality only leads to avoidance of their real purpose. Whether one views guidance as the *still, small voice within* or something connected to a unique entity from beyond makes very little difference in relationship to its usefulness. Comprehending positive guidance is the real challenge.

After seeking Guiseppe's counsel on the matter of child support, I received a startling message. I was challenged to voluntarily increase the amount by one-fifth. This sent shock waves down my spine. It was the last response I had expected, yet secretly I knew similar formulas had been passed on to many of my clients. These requests often received the same kind of objection I was raising, yet I had received hundreds of thank-you notes over the years by those who moved past the perceived mental absurdity, yielded to the requests, and experience life-changing results. I was now faced with the decision to follow the advice or concede to my resistance. Reluctantly, I wrote out the first check wondering if I had made some giant mistake and played some silly joke on myself.

For the next couple of weeks I became acutely aware of my attachments to how this money should be spent. I began to project upon my former wife and son, increasing my resentment concerning their "frivolous decisions" about his education. Slowly the awareness of my control issues reached my brain, and I was faced with this reality: for the previous few years I had been giving begrudgingly. I was not really the kind-hearted, easygoing giver I claimed to be, at least not in this category. The phony, pretentious, controlling neophyte concerning this form of giving had been exposed! It was evident that forgiveness was in order. I began to accept the rights of my son and his mother to decide how the money should be spent and how much voice I should have in the process. Concurrent in all forgiveness of others is the forgiveness of oneself. As I began to remember the personality and security needs of my former wife, it was evident why her choices were as they were. I began to accept a different point of view and moved away from the idea that mine was the only one that could possibly be right.

Not only does forgiveness of another automatically indicate forgiveness of oneself, but also the opposite is true. Every time I decided to go easy on myself regarding the recognition of an attachment concerning how my money should be spent, it paved the way for forgiveness of others. When I am more tolerant of my perceived shortcomings and devices, I automatically give others this tender treatment. Forgiveness is always a two-fold affair. When I accept my flaws, I more easily accept the flaws of others, and when I accept the flaws of others, my own are more easily understood and forgiven by me.

The measure of forgiveness is always discernible by the physical, mental and emotional reactions within an individual. Whenever distress, uneasiness, or other indicators of distrust accompany my words of proclaimed forgiveness, I have always created telltale signs in my life. Body posture--looking like I'm ready to spring into action or defend myself in the next breath--is a perfect example. The mental sign comes when internal chatter keeps asking us to review new decisions or defend old beliefs. During my two weeks of anguish and uncertainty, it was clear which side of the forgiveness fence I was really on. Each time a lie, which defends the need to hold a grudge, appears and is brought to light, clarity can take place. As I stayed open, praying only for the truth, it slowly began to penetrate my armor of resistance.

At her center, Jo Ann only wanted the best for our son. Finances were secondary to her prime objective and took a backseat in her decision-making process. I was probably jealous that she had more faith in the Universe to provide than I did concerning this matter. Prior to my review I would probably not have stumbled upon this revelation. Layers of attachment to the outcome and control of this money started to be uncovered. I faced them all and was completely exhausted once I resigned myself to the realities of my creations.

Once acceptance started, miracles began to take place. As I gave above and beyond my contractual agreement, life started smiling on me. My business increased to a record volume, and by the end of the first month I had accumulated a surplus of money even though I had volunteered to increase my monthly child support. This exercise was a wonderful reminder of what can happen when we decide to go the extra mile and give more than is required. If you're skeptical of this system and its spiritual implications, start by giving your time and talent as a beginning discipline. Wait until later, when you have experienced success, to give financially.

For now reflect on an area where you are certain that your giving is unconditional, without any strings attached. Up the ante of money, time or talent by a certain percentage, and then register both your conscious as well as subconscious reactions over a period of a week or two. The subconscious resistance will begin to surface and cause mood changes. You may grow silent, become defensive, or create an inflated ego because you've rewritten an internal program. Watch for these signs daily. Yet keep on giving even if you feel pain or experience the need to talk yourself out of it. This exercise can be humbling for even the best of unconditional givers.

Chapter Nineteen

Practice Nonverbal Communication

"Aim above morality, be not simply good, be good for something."

-Henry David Thoreau

An overemphasis on verbal communication has taken precedence in modern society. One of the most useful spiritual disciplines we can practice is learning to substitute spiritual communication for verbal communication. In this discipline the focus is on the potential creation that comes through imagery and visualization. Each time we jump into a situation orally, it can be draining. The nervous system and physical body often suffer under the undue strain that comes from the need to convince an outside party that our way, mindset, perception, or belief is right.

Jonathan comes from a dysfunctional family. Each member is in constant conflict with the others because each is trying to save the others from stupid decision-making. Each sibling, plus the remaining living parent, their mom, is in a constant battle to set the others straight and convince the others of a needed path to follow. The following is a conversation that I had with this young man. It is a classic example of how family practices get in the way of spiritual development.

I told Jonathan: "Health relates to making decisions concerning your deepest feelings. Your job, like all our jobs, is to go past the sentimental experience that we so often substitute for accurate feelings. The 'this isn't fair' experience is the sentiment, not the actual picture, of what's going on, which most perfectly paves the way to register your deepest feelings. The idea is to act from this place of accuracy, so that you are capable of accessing your spiritual feelings."

"You've shared that you reminded your family--in what you felt was a very non-critical, non finger-pointing approach--what might be good for them. I think that's very healthy. Let's get back to the unresolved pain in you, which is the pain experienced because at times you feel helpless in the art of helping others or yourself. You've cried many times that you were in excruciating physical pain and that you're unable to find the cure, the relief. You don't know how to grasp the answer or do whatever it takes to render yourself pain free."

Jonathan wanted to share what he calls his deepest beliefs about his sister Patricia and about the poor treatment she has been receiving from her daughters. They have elected to stay away from her because she is spending too much time with her ailing husband and not enough time with them. They threaten to keep the granddaughters out of the picture, depriving Jonathan's sister of enjoying them. Jonathan claims that he spoke to the daughters in a very non-critical, non finger-pointing approach. I reminded him of how healthy this can be, and I cautioned him to make sure that indeed he was coming from a non-critical approach.

I believe that the source of Jonathan's physical pain is associated with the deep psychological pain he feels because he is never quite able to "get his point across." In this case, it's with his two nieces. It is my opinion that his pain is associated with the fact that he feels helpless to solve problems, including his own. The guilt associated with this inability causes the psychological pain, which, in turn, ushers in physical discomfort. I shared with Jonathan that he can go on lashing out at people or even speaking to them in non-critical, non-confrontational ways--which he claims to have done with his nieces--and still not get results.

Jonathan's real job is accepting his limitations in helping others as well as himself when using a physical, verbal approach. My job was to share with him another way of dealing with the situation. I used the story of his sister's plight in dealing with her daughters as well as her relationship with Brian, her ailing husband.

I explained: "Our real job in the midst of all sorrow and disappointment, as well as the tragedies of life, is to keep from being swept up in them or unduly affected by them. That's a hard lesson because we're trained to be engrossed in drama. What happens is this: we eventually lose our effectiveness and are drained of all our power and energy. This is why Patricia is in the shape she's in, barely having enough energy to get by. She's not living her life. This bright, capable woman is living someone else's. If she could give permission to those around her to live their lives, she would realize that whatever drama her husband Brian has caused, he brought on himself. Is it her place to save Brian? No, it's her place to love him, not save him. Unconditional love does not create a drain on energy. It never demands from us. All it requests is: 'Be a conduit.' Being a conduit is never draining; it is life-giving. If we spend a half an hour praying for someone, envisioning his or her health without ever opening our mouths, it can possibly be the most uplifting, energizing thing we've done for him or her all day."

"Being so drained comes from ego demands. We want to be in a place of worry, struggle and pain because we are weaned on it. These ego entrapments falsely claim that help has been rendered and something constructive has been done. Millions of people perceive that if we give hell to those who have committed a crime, then we have done something powerful, good and righteous. I don't believe this. I believe that being in a state of silent witness and silent love is a miraculous, disciplined gift because we come out of it feeling good. We return, not at a loss, in despair or drained, wallowing in the mire with whomever has created his or her negative destiny, but accepting the situation at face value, as unconditionally as possible. If your sister weighs seventy-something pounds because she has worried herself into that condition, then she's a sick girl. And for you to feel sorry for her is a sick move on your part. I challenge you to think like Creator by honoring her free will and envisioning her potential bursting forth to save her. Imagine Patricia moving from co-dependency into health. That's what is going to save her and that's what is going to save you. As I'm talking about you, I'm talking about me; this truth applies to every one of us. It's called 'THE WAY.'"

"Did Jesus spend time feeling sorry for people? No, He never did. Did Jesus or Buddha spend time loving people? Yes, after their mastery, they always did. This is the difference between a master and a fool. Most of us spend our time being foolish when we're really capable of practicing mastery."

After what I considered strong language and a heavy lesson that could have turned him off, my client lovingly said, "I don't think I've ever agreed with you more and I don't think I've ever felt as much love for you as I do right now."

What are the attributes of a master? Humility, sensitivity, awareness, and deep understanding are the virtues that come to mind when I think of a master human being. Brawn is not the important ingredient here; neither is the cunning to outsmart our neighbor. What constitutes mastery is knowing when to express a perfect feeling, especially when it's nonverbal. Sitting lovingly in the presence of someone hurting, sending them lots of good will, acceptance and our faith in their abilities are often needed more than any verbal or physical display of attention we might spill onto the scene.

A master knows the importance of his or her presence, honors it humbly, and yet exhibits it as healing salve to the wounds of family, friends and associates. Masters gain strength and energy as they share unconditionally. Without this unconditional giving, every scene is fraught with deception and discrepancies. The expectation factor is obvious in Jonathan's family. He wants his nieces to change; they want their mother to change. The mother wants her husband to change, and all of them want Jonathan to change. It is evident that quality of life suffers under these conditions. My client is living in excruciating physical pain most of the time, and his sister is a seventy-five pound bundle of nerves. Both would do well to be a conduit for life's greatest force, that of unconditional love. I believe praying without attachment, envisioning without demands, and serving unconditionally are key factors to a masterful life.

On a practical level, it is essential to become a good listener if nonverbal communication is to be fully established and utilized. A good listener no longer follows an ego demand, which includes trading impressions, creating rebuttal, or engaging in endless chatter to keep the truth from being experienced from within. Whenever you find yourself wanting to express yourself this way, tell yourself: "This may well be my runaway ego needing everything to be right." Ego wants to keep us on the track of sameness and gloss over the awareness of needed change. The greatest demand of the ego is a constant demand for convenience, forever using fear to convince us so. Ego wants to promote the belief that we are here to live a convenient life. In truth we are here to live a challenging, motivated, spirited life. We have a Spirit that drives us, and the more we get in touch, the more it drives us in easy, flowing ways. Living a spirit-driven life is a magnificent assurance of being safeguarded from inconvenience because the inner strength to withstand it comes alive.

Spirit challenges us to follow and not figure out why. All will be revealed in Creator's time. Your assignment is to listen--really listen--in conversation, constantly asking yourself when the urge to speak arises, "Is my input necessary?" With time and patience you will be attuned to an inner prompting which gives the most perfect go-ahead to interject. Practice waiting for inspiration; it will come in bursts of passion, often expressing itself in words that flow out of you despite yourself. Practice waiting until exciting, enlightened conversation flows without reservation. As you slow down and refrain from talking for talking's sake or acting for action's sake, you'll be ripe for inner dialog and the feelings of what to do next. Because you're no longer busy reacting, registry of what is healthy, secure, and of Spirit flows naturally into your conscious awareness without reservation and into the lives of others.

Chapter Twenty

Safety

"If you pursue a new way of being for yourself, it will succeed. If you pursue it for others it will fail."

-Daul Yemen

Acquiring a natural feeling of safety is most important in life. Safety is a necessary ingredient to fulfilling life's purpose. Without it we stumble and die. The death I'm referring to is the death of an enjoyed life, a life without peace in the heart. Peace comes from a secure notion that all is well. Dying can take place long before we reach a state of no heartbeat. We all understand the notion of a broken Spirit, for when the Spirit no longer operates in a secure environment, it begins to withdraw. The Spirit's withdrawal constitutes premature death, a life squelched because of **fear**. Life force leaves because an individual no longer has supernatural intelligence or unconditional love in which to believe. The Spirit is broken because faith has been lost, the will to live extinguished, and the mind consumed by mass uncertainty.

In order to be safe, we must create new priorities. Spirit, which drives us, is the vehicle that makes everything possible in the physical life. Safeguarding this vehicle needs to be our number one priority. This phenomenon takes place only when we redefine the truth of our vehicle. Most of us have been groomed to believe that the mind and body vehicles operate in tandem to bring about goals and desires. What actually brings about goals and desires is **faith in our worthiness to have**, **focus on results**, and the **activation of our internal Spirit**. Why is this Spirit internal? This question will always remain a mystery. The fact does remain, though, that we have Spirit; it is the ultimate driver, and it is constantly at our disposal. The pursuit of brawn and brain is secondary to the recognition and activation of our Spirit nature.

On a regular basis I frequent health stores which often have cafes. Over fruit smoothies and rich sandwiches of organic-only ingredients, I marvel at the small talk. An exchange of conversation over the latest nutritional trends, body therapies, or alternative supplements is usually the topic at hand. This purely intellectual exchange of information concerning the physical vehicle oftentimes is the end of progress when it comes to creating safety. Belief in the ability to restore the body to a well-honed machine without the use of spiritual insight is absurd. Ultimate safety transcends the body and mind and depends, for the most part, on our state of spiritual well being.

My friend Wanda use to be a "professional" hypochondriac. She lived in excessive anxiety most of the time, fearing that she was in the middle of life-changing illnesses all the time. This woman thrived on the excitement of a new disease and the possibility of having it. Wanda believed that if she could conquer an illness, it would prove her strength by way of her ability to overcome something physical. The author of safety, Spirit, had been forgotten, and the thrill of using mental force and blatant will power to win her health became her new infatuation. Wanda eventually moved past this need to identify herself and her purpose in life with physical disability or disease. Wanda's ultimate breakthrough came when she could laugh about her own condition and at how well she had created, using mind power, the imaginary symptoms and all their ramifications. Wanda was a genius at conjuring up an image of something horrible affecting her body. Fortunately she was able to retrain her mind to focus on the creative power within for her health and well being. As she progressed, confidence for creative genius was soon unleashed in new areas.

In a recent conversation with Mattie, a first time client, she confided: "I am totally afraid of being without a husband or partner because of health problems I experienced three years ago." Her main problem stemmed from her fear to be a writer, especially of children's books. Her physical symptoms were that of vertigo, fatigue, nervous exhaustion, and depression. Mattie was in a nine-year relationship, which had run out of usefulness three years earlier. She stayed because of low self-esteem and insecurity; she stayed because of the fear of loneliness, and she stayed because she expected to receive love for all that she had given to her man Tom. He and Mattie had something in common; they both gave conditionally to each other, and, in return, each received his or her own disappointment and personal hell. Mattie's safety lay not in having someone take care of her but in Mattie's taking care of herself, which included finding the courage to write. She got sick because her inner "Golden Child" was screaming for expression. Instead of this a voice, the inner child of selfishness reigned. The difference between these two is quite simple. The Golden Child is an extension of Mattie's Spirit, the source of all creative genius, undaunted courage, and uncontaminated thought. The selfish child thrives on fear and the presumption: "I am owed something."

In this woman's case, she wants protection and safeguard in exchange for misguided subservience and allegiance. They are misguided because of their conditionality. The selfish inner child doesn't understand its power to self-protect; thus, she demands that Tom do so. The victim aspect of Mattie's personality only remembers a history of authority that was unreliable and shoved things at her as a substitute for time and attention, positive regard, or true understanding and acceptance. Consequently, Mattie wants to *stand by her man* and give him subservient attention and false allegiance because it's what she learned to give as a child. Personal power comes from the courage to accept both the fears and demands of the misguided inner one and go past them into the golden state of fearlessness. In this haven a natural power exists that returns us to God. Mattie can replace fear with courage only if she moves into a state of trust. In her case, it is trusting that self protection, coupled with Divine protection, actually exists and will squelch the fearful persuasions and demands of the internal demanding, immature voices. I assured Mattie that her sense of well being would start to emerge the more she remembered her successes in life as opposed to remembering herself as victim.

The health problems encountered by this college-educated, successful career woman exist not because she would perish if she decides to leave her partner, but because she has decided to stay. Her body, therefore, is sending a loud and clear message; **all is not well.** I tried to assure her by saying, "Nothing is wrong with this man; he just happens to no longer supply useful energy to your path."

Safety becomes the art of paying attention to the body's plea for change. Change, coming from deep within her Spirit, is called for and Mattie has many, many successes to prove that she is ready to venture out. She has, for instance, held the position of personal director for a large Boston advertising agency for the last five years. Her Golden Child is on **go**, and her body has signaled, "It's time to leave." What more reinforcement or sign could a person want?

The next time your body is reinforcing a change, be sure to give it some discerning attention. Pay attention to what persists and for how long. Notice when you keep "tripping" yourself up physically with injury from accidents or when you keep contracting illness or disease. The randomness or bad luck you presume to be the cause might not be it at all. Your body could very well be telling you that your present circumstances have outlived their usefulness and that change of job, profession, physical location, or present relationship may definitely be in order. Next, ask your Higher Self: "Is change an avoidance or attempted escape?" If you discern that it is neither, then ask yourself, "Is fear of change worth my creating negative health issues?" Very few of us, like Mattie, want the ugly results of resistance to needed life changes. Last, begin to daydream about relief in your body and what long-delayed, enjoyable activities you would be undertaking if you were free of present-day encumbrances of body and mind.

Safety comes to each of us as we create it. It often lies in knowing the gifts of Spirit, including its unending protection for those who feel worthy. Our job is to constantly discern the workings of the lower self and its lies about our culpability, especially in the arena of failure. As each of us knows and understands ourselves more and more, the risk of forgetting our talent, genius and purpose diminishes day by day. Total safety is owning and then utilizing the power that lies within. This formula ushers in a satisfaction that could possibly be the most gratifying of all.

Chapter Twenty-One

Equality: Think This Way Always

"Genius is the ability to put into effect what is in your mind."

-F. Scott Fitzgerald

Why is equality, the fine art of accepting the right of everything God has created to be O.K. with us, so essential as a spiritual discipline? Equality is how God made us to be—unified to the Creative Source. Under no circumstances does this discipline ask us to like or approve of God's creation. Equality is essential because it reinforces our stations in life. Divine Intelligence is quick to remind us that it engages only in love. Discrimination, critical judgment and segregation remain outside the realm of God's grace. Each of us has an obligation to observe our self as a part of all life. We often ostracize others because of our belief systems. Our belief tells us that we are separate and unique, which is true in part. Physically, we all live and breathe a separate humanity. We all have unique personalities, communication skills, thought patterns and personal styles. Spiritually, we are all Spirit matter, having the same Creator. Our humanity is predicated on cosmic law. The right of individuality and free will is a given under this law. Discrimination, therefore, in the eyes of God cannot be. How can a God be prejudicial concerning His or Her own creation? You ask on what premise this concept is based. I would encourage each of us to look at nature for the answer.

In nature there is an innate right to life. Within this structure, of course, there is always going to be a predator needing another life form for survival. Does nature talk back to God, claiming that one way of thinking, doing or feeling is better than another? Nature is in harmony with its surroundings; equality is the norm. Equal right to life, as well as equal right to end life, is honored by all living species except the human one.

Nevertheless, we argue the right of equality constantly among ourselves, often to the point of exhaustion. I encourage you to sit in a room full of people and observe after a short time how convoluted conversations can get. Because I was trained in psychology, I automatically notice how the emphasis slowly moves to what is wrong, unacceptable, or unappreciated concerning the conduct of other human beings. This lack of equality has become a global epidemic. Temper turns to hate and hate turns into war, all because humans forget the spiritual principle that all are equal in the eyes of Divine Love.

Watch yourself the next time you enter a room full of people. Your mind wants to either focus on your inferiority or their superiority. Maintaining a space of complete acceptance of who you are and who they are is always the challenge. Our minds automatically want to divide and segregate. What we've divided is simple. The division is between what we *perceive* they have and what we *fear* we don't have. Comparison, based on fear, takes over the peaceful mind. A fear of being criticized, blamed, or ridiculed is so ingrained that we're constantly on the defensive. We have been programmed to believe that we cannot withstand another's decision to mentally break from us. The moment we realize that the separation only exists in belief, we can easily disarm our fears. The thought of inequality can be substituted. The idea that we are all God's children, equal in His sight, can be substituted for our fearful reaction to life around us.

I was recently at a party where old fears of my inadequacy washed across my mind. I immediately asked myself why? The answer was simple: "I feel inadequate because I don't know where I stand in comparison to these other living creatures, including their ambitions, attributes and accomplishments." Instead of seeing them as spiritual beings, I wanted to differentiate them because of my perceived differences. The interesting fact remained that I didn't know if there were actual differences or not. Yet my fear arose anyway. In order to squelch my errant thought patterns, I began to review my talents. This is what I encourage all spiritual seekers to do: begin to focus on your attributes, contributions, and useful talents. It may be difficult at first, yet I encourage you to persist. Adding strong, positive feelings to the equation will also help. Soon a gentle calm will begin to resound within your consciousness. Harmony will slowly arise because the focus of your thoughts will return to what you have instead of what you "have not."

It is also very important to catch yourself when elitism wants to take over. At this point you are susceptible to the ego's demand that suggests superiority. Create a comfort zone by remembering that through the eyes of Divine Love you feel safe. Here is an exercise to help you become those eyes. Imagine that each person in the room or the auditorium is Spirit--an aspect of God in the likeness and image of God—by seeing each person reduced to a beam of light in your mind's eye. You're now envisioning the scene as if there were flashlights instead of people in front of you. Every illumination is of the same intensity, yet each is free to shine wherever he or she wants.

Reframing the scene in your mind to become a surreal portrait of what you want to believe causes change to take place more readily. Changing the mind operates best when images are projected into the process. "Flashlight beings" are neutral in most belief systems because there's very little discrimination or preference when it comes to a flashlight. The beam holds a positive image because it lights up the dark. When I saw the guests at this party as luminous light, the feeling of equality soon returned and I felt comfortable in their midst.

Try to reframe and use imagery, which is more than visualization because it includes all the five senses, whenever a "stuckness" occurs in your life. Whenever you feel either inferior or superior, know that the power to regain equality resides within. We invent the illusion of separation and inequality. By catching ourselves in the act and activating our imagination, we can quickly return to the truth. We are all equal in the eyes of love.

Chapter Twenty-Two

Prerequisites to Manifestation

"If God created us in his own image, we have more than reciprocated."

-Voltaire

"Life in the fast lane" is a common experience for most children in Western society. The art of manifestation is pushed into the lives of young, impressionable children from a very early age. Because they have the raw materials, the boon of science and technology on their side, and the free will to create, children are encouraged to build a better future. This future ranges from high degrees of comfort and material well being to the ability to maim and kill others. The encouragement to indiscriminately manifest is rampant in modern society. Manifestation, from either a scientific or spiritual definition, means the same: to make appear or to be revealed. By means of our continual focus of thought in a certain direction, creation moves from our minds into the physical world. A quick reference is to always remember: *thought precedes form.* The very nature of free will allows manifestation to take place. The acquisition and creation of our dreams, goals, and desires is all within the human framework. Because of this gift the expectation to conquer life is often the buzzword in most free countries. Spiritually speaking, the desire to unconscionably manifest is unsound, primarily because of the lack of regard for life in the outer world. With manifestation and its reality comes spiritual responsibility. This responsibility, simply stated, includes sensitivity to Mother Nature, to our fellow citizens, and to the art of being loving to all life forms.

A new global perspective is reaching epidemic proportions. It includes the assumption that scarcity prevails, and the only way to get ahead is to materialize our hearts' desires **now**. With this urgency, the desire to respect the forces outside oneself sharply diminishes. Sensitivity toward the world becomes less and less within the person in search of instant gratification. Our newspapers show signs of sociopathic behavior being more than speculation; it has reached alarming degrees of reality and popularity.

Manifestation comes with the territory of life. It is the product of free will and is always respected by the forces of the universe. I believe if Heaven were to answer all those who are perplexed by the state of affairs on the planet, its reply would be something like this: "The turbulent times you are experiencing on your planet have stemmed from an indiscriminate use of the gift of manifestation." Manifestation power, in its own right, is an energy that is equally available and totally accessible to each of us (a universal law). Compassion, understanding, and sensitivity-- the gifts of the heart--are virtues Heaven requests that we use when applying these gifts to our daily walks.

Other descriptions for manifestation include materialization, achieving a goal, obtaining an object of desire, or creating a life for ourselves. One of the best-kept secrets of our time is the fact that we create our reality. Whatever direction our most prevalent thoughts move toward eventually becomes an aspect of our reality. In truth, we have two distinct realities, spiritual as well as physical. The spiritual reality includes everything that is nonphysical. This includes thought, dreams, feelings, and imaginings. In this world lies all the raw material for manifestation. Our thoughts, prompted by the heart, solicit the Universal Mind to bring us the objects of our desires. In certain instances obstacles arise to prevent the physical manifestation. They include insincerity, half-hearted effort, lack of faith in the process, or the belief that "I can't visualize" or "I can't imagine." Any of these lacks can cause the potential to remain locked in the nonphysical world. When this happens the imagination is the only realized access point. All manifestation has a home, and the more focus on the objects of our desires, the more likely they are to reach the physical world.

The two main obstacles that prevent instant gratification or manifestation are these: experiencing a lack of deserving and a lack of focus. Lack of deserving triggers a response in us. It is about claiming our right to have. If life has taught us to feel small, unintelligent, weak, useless, petty, or untalented, we often forfeit our right to create a worthwhile existence. This lack of deserving buries itself deep in our subconscious programming. This program is often undetected by our intelligence yet is fully discernible by our actions. If we fail to hold a vision until completion, it is often because one of these "silent killers" is secretly at work and has thwarted our efforts.

The art of focus is a learned response. The earlier we teach this to ourselves, the more productive we become. Each of us has the power to imagine our goals mentally and emotionally any time we choose. Through the use of guided imagery, which includes the interjection of not only vision, but also sound, feel, smell and taste, we enhance the request. A decision to limit the involvement of our senses dilutes the signal we send to the Universal Mind. This Mind is a true respecter of our wishes and will only respond to what we most fervently desire. When the desire includes the activation of all the senses, it enhances the focus which insures a more rapid manifestation.

In order to overcome these negative obstacles--inhibited deserving and poor focusing--retraining is required. Priority must be given to the creation that we would make manifest in the physical world. Otherwise, it will stay in the nonphysical component forever. The first element of training requires that we honor the nonphysical world--this spiritual realm--as real. Validating these two realities, physical and spiritual, equally is a useful tool in getting what we want. Remember that the spiritual world contains the raw material to manifest the objects of our desires. It is also possible that it might remain the only world in which we can realize our goals. This realization takes place when we see it with our "mind's eye," "hear it in our inner mind," or "feel it within." All of us have closed our eyes and been able to look at the rooms in which we sleep or eat. They become real to us because we are envisioning the bed, dresser, wall color, shape and size of the room, or the refrigerator, cabinets and stove. We have all communicated with the inner voice or felt something so intuitive that we have known its truth without question.

Validate these realities and you're on your way, yet remember that it will always remain a mystery why some goals and aspirations never make it from the Spirit realm into the physical world.

Chapter Twenty-Three

How to Manifest

"We choose our joys and sorrows long before we experience them."

-Kahlil Gibran

The most important ingredient in the process of manifestation lies in the mindset prior to the desire. The most desirable mindset is that of peace. Peace *comes* when longing has subsided. Peace is evident when we are detached from an outcome. Whenever clients come to me frustrated because their long-standing goals continually lie just out of reach, I always remind them that being satisfied in the moment is the great prerequisite to accomplishing any worthwhile goal. "Why is this so important?" my client may ask. My reply is always the same: "Negative dissatisfaction breeds inconsistency." Dissatisfaction tells us conclusively that we have lost track of the moment. We're somewhere out in the future fretting about what has yet to materialize instead of staying consistently focused on our goal.

I recently had a discussion with a man concerning the concept of "accepting what is." He completely failed to grasp the idea, claiming that if he did not adhere to dissatisfaction, he would not be standing his ground or upholding his rights. I began to realize the language barrier that existed between us. We finally came to the conclusion that we were talking about the same thing. When I interjected the word *reality* into my equation, he completely understood. In essence, if the reality of things around us can be accepted at face value, we are, in effect, accepting what is. By opposing ultimate reality we have started a war which is always impossible to win.

Peace only comes when the heart and head are in agreement that somehow mysteriously and miraculously things are as they should be spiritually. Ultimate reality is the sum total of all thought, as well as its manifestation called the material world. The war begins inside of us when we confuse accepting and agreeing. Accepting in no way implies that we have to agree with an aspect of life. Disagreeing with a position is a human right. Disagreement, like agreement, is part of the free will process. Acceptance, on the other hand, is the foundation for all change. Change in the form of manifestation comes most easily when we accept our life and everything in it at face value prior to a desired outcome.

Most clients are stumped by this philosophy; they assume that dissatisfaction is the great motivator of change. Spirituality tells us that acceptance contains the raw material that leads to faster and more useful changes in our lives. Dislike for something can be a powerful motivator in the world of change. When we register a discomfort in our emotional world, it is often an indicator that change is knocking at the door. Peace and dissatisfaction are not incompatible. This condition is the perfect medium for going inward and seeking higher guidance. Dissatisfaction, devoid of disgust, is the foundation for positive emotional display in the art of manifestation. If our emotional life is filled with trust, openness, optimism and satisfaction, then the likelihood of quicker manifestation occurs. This fertile ground of change, charged with positive regard for life, is more likely to yield results than the barren soil of regret stemming from disappointment and disgust, which prompts lack of acceptance.

The perfect example of experiencing dissatisfaction yet staying in a place of acceptance occurred to me recently. I attended a concert of two legends, Bob Dylan and Paul Simon. Our seats were very good, and my companion and I were prepared for an auspicious evening. Just into the second song, four rambunctious concert-goers stood up, letting themselves be enthralled by the music. They just happened to be two rows in front of us. Immediately two men, who were right behind them and directly in front of us, joined in the celebration. As I looked around I noticed that these were the only six people standing in our section of the amphitheater.

A few loud comments by those around us, directing these energetic patrons to sit down, were to no avail. They were entranced by their musical heroes and therefore oblivious to everyone sitting behind them experiencing inconvenience. I was dissatisfied and I began to register reactions in my body. My companion, obviously more spiritually attuned in that moment than I, just sat there unaffected. An intellectual wave of small talk began immediately inside of me. It was trying to blame, needing to punish, and wanting someone to do something about the situation. Just before my anxiety reached my forehead, I caught myself. In that instant, I was keenly aware of my lack of acceptance of the situation that life was presenting to me at that moment. My thoughts had been on the cost of the ticket and how little value I was receiving for my money. My thoughts focused on those inconsiderate "dummies" who were showing absolute lack of regard for others. In this brilliant instant, I realized that I was in charge of my life, and I was the only one who could do anything about my problem. I realized this: basing my decision to act upon a need to get even was ludicrous.

Spiritually speaking, the problem resided only within my belief system. My dissatisfaction, which had turned negative, came from my thoughts, which then triggered my emotions. By thinking again from a viewpoint of acceptance, I was able to return to equilibrium. I honored my frustration, anxiety, and anger. It was real and it was very much happening to me. What then is a person to do when he or she is caught in the trap of wanting and needing to take action and desiring to remain spiritually attuned at the same time?

I took some deep breaths, releasing the stress caused by being mad. I imagined the stress slowly draining downward from my forehead towards my feet. I envisioned degrees of letting go, focusing on openings in the soles of my feet and watching with my mind's eye as the energy of discontent slowly drained from my body. This would be similar to opening a pop bottle, turning it upside down, and watching the fluid spill out onto the floor. Within a very short time I returned to the musicians, laughing inside at my folly and deciding that I wanted to enjoy this evening. Between songs I found myself tapping courteously on the shoulder of the man in front of me and asking him as politely as I could if he would simply look around, especially to his rear, the next time a fast song started playing. I encouraged him to notice that no one behind his row was standing and that he might be blocking the view of many. I also asked him to consider my feelings because I was having an internal issue. I explained that I had not anticipated spending $75 to view his butt!

From that moment on I was fine; I had voiced politely my dissatisfaction and was attempting to the best of my ability to return to a place of universal acceptance of what was happening, not to me, but in life around me. I was also painfully reminded of how much in charge I am of what is happening *to me*. I was choosing to return to peace and it felt good. I was also back in the manifestation mode, able to call on the universal raw material as my aid and Universal Intelligence as my guide. My friend stayed consistently positive in attitude and acceptance, helping me avoid the pitfall of complaining out loud. It was obvious, even though unspoken, that we both had decided to hold the vision of our views somehow becoming miraculously unobstructed. The evening, from then on, turned out to be a splendid event. The original four eventually decided to dance in the aisles, and because they were no longer an obstruction, the two men immediately in front of us chose to remain seated.

Life will respond in like manner to our thoughts and emotional displays. As the early Christian disciple Mark puts it: "Again amen, I say to you if two of you agree on earth about anything for which you pray, it shall be granted to them by my heavenly Father." As I let go of anxiety, stress, and belief that my rights had been violated, I was able to attract to me the situation I wanted. Universal Intelligence somehow mysteriously impacted the conscience of those who had been my irritants. On a telepathic level they received our request because, on my part, I eventually accepted the reality we were experiencing, owned my dissatisfaction, and put my trust in the ability to manifest.

Chapter Twenty-Four

Look to Nature

"The living self has one purpose only: to come into its own fullness of being, as a tree comes into full blossom, or a bird into spring beauty, or a tiger into lustre."

-D. H. Lawrence

The most important aspect of nature is this; she is the most perfect symbol for growth and prosperity we have. Nature offers us constant examples of ebb and flow, change of seasons, and complete synchronicity. One purpose of nature is what I call accepting growth. Nature seems to accept all of its patterns and basic instincts, which sustain life. I know of no other realm of life that offers so many useful examples for human beings to stay balanced and healthy.

When I spend time in nature, it is as if timelessness and expansiveness take over. Nature is in no hurry; she is totally accepting of what will come, yet nature can be on full alert in the face of impending danger. She is acutely attuned to climactic changes, the invasion of predators, or the need to take full advantage of rain after a long dry spell.

Nature's no fool because her antennae are always up. She follows a keen sense of direction from the deep place of inner knowing. This is why she is such a great model when it comes to the spiritual walk. If our antennae were as good as nature's, we could easily safeguard ourselves from the pitfalls of life. When we act as responsibly as nature, sensing danger becomes as natural as breathing.

When the Aborigines of Australia undertake a walk, they safeguard themselves and their mission by replicating what nature has taught them. Each of their thoughts is dutifully compliant with nature's way so that they walk in harmony with their surroundings. The Aborigines' profound communion with nature has been cultivated by centuries of practicing telepathy. This advanced culture needs very little verbal interaction for they literally know how to comprehend each other without words. Their rapport with nature is equally fascinating. Often in the middle of the desert, when they need water, one of the elders will put his ear to the ground, able to detect an underground stream. Another elder comes behind them puncturing the sand until the stream is found. After clearing a hollow reed of debris, they are able to suck out the water and replenish themselves. The Aboriginal people are also adept at observing from a distance the vapor that pools of water give off as well as being able to smell and feel a hidden supply in the breeze. Whenever surface water has been found, these in-tune individuals simply wait in hiding until a thirsty animal comes to drink from the small oasis. Dinner's main course has just arrived.

One of my past hobbies was trail hiking in the Appalachian Mountains. On one excursion to a terrific waterfall in North Georgia, my friend Albert and I experienced firsthand a deep communion with nature. I wanted to take a shortcut to the falls trail. It was a short distance of about a mile. This side trail was little used because the main entrance was in another location. My desire to take this shortcut backfired for we got totally lost in the face of impending nightfall. By the time we entered the main trail that passed by the waterfall, it was dark so I decided to start practicing a technique for staying balanced that I had learned while hiking the Inca Trail in Peru.

My friend and I put our hands out, palms down, toward the earth. We imagined that our fingers were sensing the trail and that somehow we would receive guidance in a radar-like fashion. We focused on the trail, narrow as it was, and created trust that our feet would be guided along it. We kept listening for the sound of the waterfall, yet never heard it. After treading gingerly for what seemed like miles, we decided to stop for the night on what appeared to be a flat surface. As I was exploring this small area for a likely place to pitch our tent, the need for an abrupt halt washed over me. Just as the animal kingdom constantly receives the vibration of impending danger, so did I. I instinctively knew to go no further and swung around sharply to inform my hiking buddy. As I turned, I noted a shift in my backpack but was not able to pinpoint what may have occurred because of the darkness. Without knowing why, I informed my friend that this place was inappropriate for us and we must move on. Up the trail a little further we found an overhang where the rock jetted out to form a canopy of protection in case of rain. Two exhausted campers were ready to pitch their tent. To my amazement, the tent that I started out with was no longer attached to my gear. Where was it? Then I remembered my quick turn and the strange sensation with my backpack. In that moment I realized what had happened. My tent had ejected itself by sliding through the straps that held it in place.

Exasperated, yet still somewhat elated because we had traversed the narrow trail so well, we were ready for sleep. We laid our sleeping bags under the jutting cliff and prayed for sleep. The next morning our eyes revealed the startling details of our adventure the night before. To our amazement, there was very little on the north side of the trail in the way of terra firma. We were aghast at the steep descent of the hillside. One errant step and one or both of us could have careened down a very steep slope. Because we had acted in accordance with nature, we were spared potential harm. We stayed focused, accepted our plight, remained calm, and trusted our internal radar.

We were astonished to find out that the potential spot for setting up our tent was the top of a rock. On three sides of the rock there was a cliff that looked out over a seventy-five-foot drop. Had I not swung around when I felt the internal urge to stop, I would have surely ended up like my tent-- seventy-five feet below. It had slipped right out of my backpack, and because it fell so far down, we never heard the sound it made as it crashed against the ground. Amazed at the startling revelations and thankful we had emulated nature's great design, at last we were on our way to the waterfall. We walked in silent meditation pondering what could have been and thankful for what was. We were safe in the loving arms of nature.

Nature is full of abundance if we only stop to observe. I marvel every time I hike the mountain trails observing the vegetation residing in the barren crevices of rock cliffs. Trees, though sometimes stunted and scraggly, grow in the most unlikely of places. Seeds scattered with only a few inches of nurturing topsoil can produce the most amazing results. Our abundance is like this because all of us are carved from the same design as the rest of nature. Our curse or glory, however we choose to define it, is in the fact that we can measure our talent and flourish in the most unlikely of places.

Nature surrenders herself to the Life Force that created it. We have the same choice, but few elect it. Nature lives in abundance because she does not know the concept of being without. If a seed dies because of lack of nutrients or water, it accepts its fate without question. The seed probably knows that it has thousands of brothers and sisters waiting to land in a better place eager to propagate the species.

Humans often live in fear because their plight might be like life on the cliff with only a small snatch of nurturing available to them. Humans fear death because they have been taught that life is a onetime experience. The animal kingdom hears its predators and at the same time accepts the game of life. If an animal outruns its prey, it is granted the gift of life for another day. If it is caught in the jaws of some hungry species slightly higher up the food chain, then it resigns itself to a perfect death. Death is no burden to the creature that operates by perfect instinct and timing which, by the way, is the ultimate goal of spirituality. Abundance is the ability to live fearlessly without the encumbrances of the human mind which is not always so accepting.

Nature accepts her cyclical way. Trees, animals, and plants know instinctively that a new season will bring change to the environment. The game of life to them is one of pure growth. They do their part in the grand scheme of things by maturing and being a source of life in the forest. The leaves fall and decay to become a blanket of rich fertile topsoil in which seeds are nurtured abundantly and grow plentifully. What was once jagged rock with only smatterings of life-giving soil now has become an abundant carpet for all plant life. Nature seems to look forward to each new season as either a time of replenishment or rest.

In our frenzied world these two abundantly necessary ingredients--action (replenishment) and reflection (rest)--appear obsolete to the masses. The motto, "I want my fair share yet I don't necessarily want to work for it," is embraced by millions of youth across our planet. Their actions have been misguided and maligned because they so often choose the actions of negative persuasion and misguided energy. In my global travels, I observe young people weaned on receiving handouts because their parents wanted to insure for them a better life than they had been brought up with. In theory it sounds wonderful, but the plain truth remains: handouts have their drawbacks and are contrary to the law of cause and effect. Unconditional giving, on the other hand, is part of our obligation as spiritual citizens of earth. We are to share and trust that in our sharing, we do not diminish our fortune, but, in actuality, increase it. This kind of action is in perfect resonance with nature.

A handout based on sympathy shows lack of trust in the recipient of our gift. This kind of handout is an example of unhealthy replenishment, which is contrary to nature. A healthy one is based on an empathetic urge manifesting from the heart center. In the state of healthy reflection (rest) this is what happens. Our job is to have faith in the ability of another, teach through the example of reaching our goals, and share examples of how the universal storehouse has been our source. When we teach our youth to replenish their lives by trusting the Universal Forces that govern all life, we've set a far better example, thus reducing fear-based mentality. Fear that drives parents to overly protect their children is a very debilitating premise upon which to raise them.

Teaching abundance generates far more success when teaching our children to become successful, self-reliant adults.

My own brother is a perfect example of being empowered by a well-meaning but misguided parent. My father taught my brother at an early age the negative value of money. He would constantly bail my brother out when he was in financial difficulty. My dad was just beginning to earn a living when the Great Depression hit, so he had felt the ravaging effects of poverty firsthand. He was also orphaned at the age of thirteen by the premature deaths of both his mother and father. My dad adopted a subconscious program that constantly encouraged him to safeguard anyone in need. He genuinely believed that he was doing my brother a favor each time he would financially bail him out. It wasn't until twenty-five years later that my father realized the error of his ways. Instead of empowering my brother, each dole whittled away his self-esteem and integrity. The debilitating effects of these actions caused this vibrant, talented young man to have such permanent psychological as well as physical impairment that he succumbed to death at the early age of forty-eight. By this time he had given up alcohol and chemical dependency, yet his body was no match for these long-standing addictions.

Nature would never signal to one of her own: "I am scared for you." She would instead honor one's right to be, to grow, to thrive, and to become the tallest tree on the hill. Each new seed knows instinctively that it has a chance to be the perfect specimen of its species. Spirituality says that we contain all the inherent material to make a useful and lasting impression on the world.

Christian scripture says that we are never given more than we can handle. So why are some humans so fearful while others attempt to weather the storms of life, endure pain, or live with disappointment? In observing my father over the course of my lifetime, I believe that he was out of touch with the cyclical nature of life. Nature represents natural order, a way of doing business with life based on trust.

My dad has dealt with trust issues all of his life. Everything he held dear as a child was swept away--his mother when he was eight and his father when he was thirteen. This left him in a state of uncertainty and distrust with obvious abandonment issues. His subconscious belief formulated the premise: if you love something, look out, for it will surely disappear before your eyes. Whenever he saw a family member in pain over a loss, his mind automatically reverted to the past, and he felt sympathy for whoever was experiencing hurt. His internal program was screaming, "Help them cut their losses for it is not fair for someone to go through what I encountered." The spiritual way teaches us that we have far more resilience, endurance, and strength that we can imagine.

All of us can look at the times when we have been down and out, broken and suffering because of a perceived loss. During some of this loss time we may have wondered, "How will I ever survive and regain the will to carry on?" In hindsight, we can reflect on having come full circle, recovered from our loss, returned to daily life, and found happiness once again. Replenishment and strength come when we observe our track record and notice how successfully we again and again recover from loss, suffering and pain. With this awareness, we can stop falling in the rut of taking handouts as a cure and tap into our endless potential as human beings. It was only after my father said, "No more," did my brother begin his slow and often tumultuous road to mental and emotional stability--albeit too late to save himself.

Besides nature being synonymous with the fertile ground of replenishment, she also holds the secret of rest. Sleep is a natural means of getting rest so that the body is restored to full physical strength. Nature has natural cycles of rest, which can be observed every time we are out in her bounty. A simple stroll through the park, with the added pleasure of resting on a bench, might be a simple reminder that we need to observe life from the vantage point of rest. The first important measure to notice is the lack of disagreement between all the elements of nature. There is no apparent fight between the blades of grass concerning who is to grow the tallest and reach for the sun the fastest. Observe the animal kingdom closely and you might see stages of hibernation: cocoons in spring or fall, spiders idly basking in the sun just waiting for their prey, or an egret with its wings outstretched drying in the sun after a morning dip to retrieve its breakfast.

Go even deeper into the observation and you'll find mindsets different than your own. The mind of nature seems to be totally in a state of peace and harmony with its surroundings. From this observation you can learn a great lesson. All our stress and anxiety can be reduced if we but follow this simple example. After a walk in the woods we return more tranquil. Why does this phenomenon occur? The answer is simple; there is no war in nature. Nature accepts life on her own terms, on Creator's terms, so why would we argue with this formula? It has taken this planet through cycle after cycle of successful evolution. After billions and billions of years, the planet is still going strong, rearranging itself after glacial meltdowns, blackouts from meteorite invasion, and animal extinction. Creation just keeps moving forward with new cycles of replenishment and rest; it never questions itself or its motives. Spiritual disciplines ask that we do the same--accept life on an "as is" basis. When this occurs we allow the mind to rest more and more. Any attempt at lack of acceptance of this fact moves us from a place of internal rest to a place of disharmonious thought.

What often comes to mind when I'm trying to return to a place of acceptance, where the mind can rest in peace, is a line from the *Course In Miracles*. It asks, "Do I want to be right or do I want to be happy?" I've used this simple line thousands of times to return to a place of natural order. Nature seems to be completely beyond the need to be right, and what I observe of her is this; she is perfectly happy and content just the way she is. My need to be right comes from aggravation in my mind. When I can pinpoint this aggravation and squelch its haunting demands, I once again return to a place of equilibrium. I recommend to all of us that time in nature become the great example for life at its finest.

Simple ways to stay connected with nature are always at hand. Put a vase of flowers on your desk. Allow pastoral settings to hang on your walls. Open a window from time to time and breathe in fresh air or buy a desk fountain and relax. If you're really adventurous, spend a weekend in the woods. When you do, bring back mementos like pinecones, meaningful stones, or flowers that you can press between the pages of a book. If you are truly an indoor person, look out the window from time to time to see if birds are flying. Notice the wind catching the leaves in the trees or wait dutifully for the sky to become radiant as the sun begins to set. In native indigenous cultures, the appearance of an animal on the landscape is often taken as a sign of direction, a gift from Great Spirit.

While meditating in one of Peru's most sacred spots, a giant candelabra carved into the side of a great hill near the Nasca Plains, I saw a yellow bird. The bird flew from my left to my right in one of the most powerful visions I'd ever received. The bird was like a canary yet it looked wild and untamed. As I began to uncover this mystery through research about the color and the symbolism of birds, I was able to discern my gift from Mother Nature. The bird represented a need to follow my creative instincts from a place of gut-level intuition.

Years later, I used this scene on the cover of my first commercially produced audiocassette that became part of a *Flight to Freedom* series. The rocks, trees, animals, wind, clouds, fire, mountains, plains, streams, fields, and flowers all have meaningful significance and can aid us in the restoration of our own natural order.

The significance of nature's symbols is often hidden in our collective unconscious minds. In DNA we carry the energy, traits and memories of our ancestors. This internal activity is often the basis of a deja vu experience. In times past, others have used these symbols in ritual and ceremony for empowerment and to pay homage to the gods. Imprints of these experiences are accessible to us in the collective unconscious. Often an instant intuitive "hit" or insight is available to us when nature speaks. Our job is to pay attention, accept the gift, research what it has meant to others, and search for a personal message designed just for us.

Chapter Twenty-Five

Ultimate Forgiveness

"Forgiveness is the answer to the child's dream of a miracle by which what is broken is made whole again, what is soiled is made clean again."

-Dag Hammarskjöld

The most important ingredient in any successful life is forgiveness. It is the "soap of life," and with it we are washed clean. Ultimate spirituality speaks of only one kind of God--the God of love. In modern Western society we have tried to intellectualize love. This limitation creates great disharmony within Western worship and religion. Knowing and feeling absolute trust for this Force is true salvation.

Trust comes about when we decide to forgive Creator for the unhealthy creations surrounding us. Our logic is based on the fact that we see destruction everywhere; our flaw is that we deem this destruction, which is caused by a presumably benevolent or loving Father, to be evil and uncalled for. From a standpoint of truth, all creation comes from the ashes of destruction. Old beliefs must die for us to grow spiritually. Life comes and goes as it is intended to, according to natural cycles. Death and destruction make way for new life without exception.

Our job is to reevaluate what we term evil and understand the intended nature of all destruction. The science of forestry has shown us conclusively that forest fires constitute a thinning process, destroying the old and making room for new growth. Destruction, according to spiritual values, means nothing more than change. The God of love obviously advocates change because if we look closely at any facet of life--any part of the animal, mineral, or plant kingdoms--we observe growth only by change.

What seems obvious to our logical mind is often in opposition to authentic life. Divine Creator and His or Her creation will always appear mysterious to the finite mind. We tend to condemn what we fail to understand. I believe the greatest mistake we can make as humans is to hold a grudge against Creator. So often I find this problem at the root of my clients' mental stuckness. Sometimes I hear these words: "I can't take it anymore. I'm so sick and tired of this world; I just want to leave." This attitude reflects a deep-seated hatred for a God who apparently allows havoc, destruction, or death at any second. The keyword in the sentence is *allows*. The logical mind finds a loving God only capable of love, so how could He allow such horrendous, untimely destruction to strike mercilessly at the heart of human existence? If I told you, as I have told thousands of clients, that He did not invent the destruction, you'd think me daft. Yet it is one way of looking at a mental solution for this internal dilemma. Perhaps because of the gift of free will, our energy sets in motion the destructiveness of life. Does God snatch us into the Spirit realm without respect for life? I do not believe so. Free will allows us to preprogram something as precious as our own life as well as our death. Negative self-talk that keeps encouraging us to leave needs to be considered in the equation of life. We've often heard the line, "Be careful what you ask for." When a client keeps up the internal chatter, as well as the external declaration, "I just want to die," it just very well may be an actual predictor of his own fate.

To blame the God of Creation for all of the mishaps, accidents, and "premature" deaths is a wrongful indictment. If we started looking for the actual perpetrator of the crime, we might begin to see human involvement at work. Perhaps we, by infusing ourselves with anger, greed, hatred, and lack of forgiveness, set up patterns and vibrations that can destroy life itself. Perhaps in a state of wisdom, an elder who is tired and ready to go home wills his own death.

In 1987, I was sitting on an airplane beside two missionaries. The three of us were headed for Brazil. They were returning to work in a remote village in the Amazon while I was headed to an institute designed to foster spiritual development. During the course of our conversation, these two men shared a piece of their story. They would go into a selected village, learn the spoken language of the people, create an alphabet, teach them to read, then attempt to convert them to Christianity. The length of time to complete this process took about seven years. These two men were starting their second assignment in a brand new village, both into their eighth year, in Brazil.

Since I have always been fascinated with undisturbed, indigenous people, I was eager to hear their stories of tribal life. One such story involved an elder tribesman whom they met on the first day of their mission stay. He appeared pleasant, dignified and wise. He shared, "I will be returning to my hut now to go to sleep." After about four days, one of the missionaries inquired about the whereabouts of this kindly elder. They were told that he passed on to the Spirit world just as he had promised. Because of a language barrier, the missionaries assumed that he was going to take a nap. His intended communication was to announce his upcoming death. It was a startling revelation for these two because the reality struck at the heart of their Christian upbringing and vocational endeavor. They had no idea of the power of the mind and the unlimited number of choices humans actually have. It was a true culture shock for them to be exposed firsthand to someone who wills his own death. Through observation of Christian scripture, we get a clear indication that Jesus knew of his impending death and honored his role by not resisting it. This text tells us that even though He did not will it, He was, nonetheless, capable of honoring the One who did.

Choosing to leave is a common practice honored in many North American native tribes as well. My point is that we have more control over death that we want to realize and with some in-depth anthropological investigation, we can easily validate its occurrence. Just as this native Brazilian chose willingly to leave, millions more are also choosing death without their even knowing it. Our minds move in the direction of our most pertinent thoughts. If we keep telling ourselves, and others, that we want to die, in essence, we are inventing our destiny. A death program impregnated deeply enough in our subconscious can create its reality. Be careful what you ask for.

The spiritual pilgrim begins to venture slowly into the cracks of his resistance and notices how in control of life he actually is. When this is not remembered, it is easy to make God our scapegoat, which breeds a deep, resounding grudge for His lack of benevolence and mercy. It is easy to be brainwashed into a mindset of thinking we are helpless and not in control. What then is the Divine role in the overall scheme of our lives? It is always the same; we are loved by Infinite Divine Intelligence without conditions of any kind. God will not show favoritism by allowing some actions and prohibiting others. Free will is His obvious choice for us. We have the power to create or destroy lives, including our own. It is true; Divine Creator (omniscience) did invent and obviously allows evil (omnipotent), yet we have the power to include or delete these destructive forces from our lives (free will).

Once our role is understood from a soul perspective, we begin to formulate new plans of action for our lives, as well as new understandings of the Divine Nature. Creator will never ban our creative power and ability nor will this Power accept responsibility for our doings. In essence, we need to forgive ourselves for blaming God and start taking responsibility for our lives. The only harm done is believing that our God is one of wrath. As we begin to understand the deeper nature of God's role in His universe, we come to the conclusion that this power has never wronged us. The only misfortune we create is the one created by our minds and negative emotions which construct the idea and destructive belief that our God is one of indiscriminate destruction.

Ultimate forgiveness means to forgive God in whatever form you define this absolute power. If you believe He is a destroyer and cannot figure out why He destroys, forgive

Him anyway. If you believe in the God of infinite wisdom, which includes the invention of negative, destructive thoughts that can be turned into reality, forgive Him anyway. If you believe in an absolute benevolent God who is giving you free will, and you take responsibility for all you've created, forgive yourself for perhaps you are a god too.

Chapter Twenty-Six

Quality of Life

"Very little is needed to make a happy life."

-Marcus Aurelius

My vision is that each person who has come in contact with this book has been able to understand, more fully than when we began, just what God has to do with a healthy, quality life. We have moved through chapter after chapter describing sometimes stuck participants in the play of life. By now you can probably identify with some of the same stuckness. All of these characters had one thing in common; they lacked discipline. Each one neglected in some damaging way to reprogram the subconscious mind, discern the inner voice, or formulate a more perfect image of God. Through ignorance or unhealthy manipulation, these children of Divine Creator forgot over and over again their most powerful resource, a source of infinite, unfathomable love, a subject of faith, a provider of raw materials, and a co-creator of our every wish. On a more perfect note, this Universal Force wants to share its perfect Intelligence in every moment of our lives and constantly remind us when we stray from our unique purpose or our ability to be unconditionally giving and loving.

The disciplines of spirituality are often so simple that they are overlooked in lieu of more complicated, sophisticated or intellectual ways of achieving quality life. I have attempted to show again and again the holistic approach to successful living. Each of us faces pain and suffering as well as hardship and distress. We can use these simple spiritual principles and techniques to guide us through the discomforts and diseases of the mind, body or emotions, or we can ignore them and prolong our suffering and delay relief. The spiritual principles and applied disciplines are pathways leading back to the truth of not only our unique beings but to the exact nature of the Universe itself. Time and time again throughout this book, you are given explicit descriptions of the symptoms, sometimes permanent, of those who failed to align with their purpose and personal mission. The price that these people paid can be avoided. Pay attention to your body signals, give credence to the insights that come from uncontaminated intuition and learn to trust the constant stream of signs you receive from nature. These revelations are as thirst quenching to your higher conscience as sipping cold spring water on a steamy summer's day.

Symptoms are indicators that stirrings from a soul level are being received by the body-mind. If we are disciplined in the art of quiet and stillness (being), then our chances of understanding and correcting our symptomatic conditions increase. As I have pointed out, if we can ascertain the block in consciousness that has helped create the errant subconscious program, then chances are correction can be obtained. Mental refocus was often part of the assignment given to many of my clients. I trust that insights concerning your own blocks have been uncovered through the tales of peril incurred by my clients. I also hope the stories of success based on faith in the spiritual process and of faith in a Higher Power have been uplifting.

It has also been my intention to give fresh exposure to the concept of the spiritual journey. The concept, relationship with, and identification of God have been a continuing process in the evolution of mankind. If we trace the steps over the last few thousand years, we can easily say that the face of God has changed many times. There has been a constant argument in theological circles concerning the most elevated way to find and know God. The argument about whether the rational or mystical approach is the best way has been ongoing. Part of my attempt in this book has been to show the unmistakable negative effects on the psyche of those who have been persuaded to overindulge in the one or the other. I've attempted to explain the need for balance between the heart and the head when it comes to seeking, knowing, following, and ultimately surrendering to Divine Intelligence.

Too often, because of religious indoctrination and overstressed dogma, pathways to God have been a turnoff for the wounded or disillusioned pilgrim. Today, because we are recovering from the Dark Ages, we are too savvy and streetwise to be held captive by overpowering religious traditions that tend to constrict and condemn instead of extol human virtues and encourage expansion of consciousness. The simple yet effective lessons taught here are to encourage faith in an accepting Universe, a loving Creator and a set of principles that I believe are foolproof. My prayer is that this material, if nothing else, has been a vehicle to reawaken inquisitiveness and spark your interest concerning less traditional approaches to the spiritual journey.

I've also shown how love, as opposed to fear, as a prime motivator can make the journey through life far more enjoyable and easy on the senses. Instead of looking for the God of wrath and vengeance around every corner, my clients are encouraged to look and expect love and acceptance. Many have shunned this idea condemning it as overly simplistic. It has often taken months and months of encouragement to help a person think more positively, optimistically and bravely concerning his or her fate in life. Yet, as the mind goes, so follow the senses. Clients have, just as you can, implemented simple, basic spiritual instructions so that the intellect understands the origin of safety, the body feels secure and alive, and all emotional display is registered and accepted. In the future whenever a particular problem or negative pattern haunts you, consider picking up this manuscript and turning to the chapter that may help steer you back on course.

For myself the experience of sharing the Universal Way has been a lifesaver. With my stubbornness and illusionary capability, I would not be following my truth as faithfully without thousands of hours of sharing as a teacher and counselor. I am able to understand right along with my audience the nature of a poor choice and what can be done once I have blundered. Remember that the information you have witnessed has been a condensed version of so many, many hours of exposure to both spiritual dysfunction and the road to freedom. I thank my spiritual guidance for its constant input and clarification of the truth. I feel privileged to be able to sense another's subconscious program, share the information of what is both working and not working, and allow a prescription for a better future to flow out of me. I also thank the Spirits of the departed for impressing upon me their thoughts so that the bereavement process needed by their loved ones here on earth becomes a useful step towards closure and healing.

Experiencing something is the best way to place it in our world of definition and context. Look, listen and try to feel the experience of the Divine in every undertaking of your life. By doing so you'll automatically be one step closer to staying in the flow. It may take awhile to wean yourself from the traumas and dramas of everyday life, yet peace beyond understanding has more health than you will ever know until you choose to experience it. I encourage you not to wait until you need a medical procedure, psychiatric care or the deathbed experience to improve the quality of your life. Pay attention to the *still, small voice*, strive to remember your purpose, and be sensitive to life through acceptance and understanding. With this in mind you'll never forget what God's got to do with it. Amen.